CHAMPION BLOKES learn to LOVE

IAN 'WATTO' WATSON

WATTO BOOKS

A book by Watto Books
© Ian Watson 2017

Apart from any fair dealing for the purposes of private study, research, criticism or review as permitted under the Copyright Act, no part of this book may be reproduced by any process without the written permission of the publishers.

Some names are changed to protect the privacy of individuals.

Watto Books, PO Box 241, Woody Pt QLD 4019, Australia

thechampionsguide.com

ISBN: 978-0-9873788-3-5

Scripture quotations marked NIV and NIV84 are taken from the HOLY BIBLE, NEW INTERNATIONAL VERSION® NIV®. Copyright © 1973, 1978, 1984 by Biblica, Inc.™. Used by permission of Biblica, Inc. ™. All rights reserved worldwide. "NIV" and "NEW INTERNATIONAL VERSION" are trademarks registered in the United States Patent and Trademark office by Biblica, Inc.™.

Scripture quotations marked AMP are taken from the Amplified Bible, Copyright © 1954, 1958, 1962, 1964, 1965, 1987 by The Lockman Foundation. Used by permission.

Scripture quotations marked ESV are taken from The Holy Bible, English Standard Version® (ESV®) Copyright © 2001 by Crossway, a publishing ministry of Good News Publishers. All rights reserved. ESV® Text Edition: 2016

Scripture quotations marked MSG are taken from THE MESSAGE, copyright © 1993, 1994, 1995, 1996, 2000, 2001, 2002 by Eugene H. Peterson. Used by permission of NavPress. All rights reserved. Represented by Tyndale House Publishers, Inc.

Scripture quotations marked NLT are taken from the Holy Bible, New Living Translation, copyright ©1996, 2004, 2007, 2013, 2015 by Tyndale House Foundation. Used by permission of Tyndale House Publishers, Inc., Carol Stream, Illinois 60188. All rights reserved.

Scripture quotations marked TPT are from *Proverbs: Wisdom from Above* and *The Psalms: Poetry on Fire*, The Passion Translation®, copyright © 2014. Used by permission of BroadStreet Publishing Group, LLC, Racine, Wisconsin, USA. All rights reserved.

Scripture quotations marked KVJ are taken from the King James Version, public domain.

Editing, illustration and design Belinda Pollard

Copy editing Alix Kwan

Cover signwriting James Marsh & Chad Polinski, Eternal Signs

Cover photography Peter Jendra

Reactions to
Champion Blokes Learn to Love

Watto takes it to a new level in his latest book, and every bloke (and Sheila for that matter) will be better off for reading it. From the moment I started, I was drawn in by Watto's honesty and vulnerability and his trademark way of saying things just as they are. Watto gets to the guts of what matters most in the universe and *Champion Blokes Learn to Love* is easily the best book for Aussie men that has been written on this eternally significant subject. Read it and give it to your sons, brothers, dads, husbands, uncles and mates to read it too, because we will all be better off when we take these nuggets of truth to heart and become fair dinkum about putting them into practice. Paul Morrison, West Coast Eagles Chaplain, Shed Happens WA

The world is a better place coz Watto's at it again putting his vapours on the paper. I'm so glad you've written this book. The Big Fella's going to use this to speak into hearts – old, hard, craggy, young, ambitious, arrogant, all of them – and mound them into His heart, the eternal heart of the ultimate loving Big Fella! Michael Knight, Peer Power

This book is such a practical handbook on how to make your relationship amazing. Watto raises topics people might be hesitant to discuss but he does it in a gentle, caring way. His wisdom is born of life experiences and he draws from a variety of real-life marriages to teach. The tone is relatable, conversational, and the book makes you feel excited to use the tools to experience change in your own relationship. We love that the motivating factor is not shame but encouragement, and no-one goes backwards with encouragement. Dan & Emma Willmann

It's a great book, Watto, and I believe that God will use it to change this nation. Practical, helpful advice that is lacking in today's society. Rachel & Paul McLaughlin

This is Watto's best writing thus far. He's nailed it – super topic, message delivered in his signature style, straight to the point, digestible Aussie language that can be read by all. Best of all, he has the essence of relationship issues/struggles/solutions all together in a little book that points to the bigger Book and its Author, who made us all to be in amazing relationships. Lenore Hall

I have been Watto's accountant for over 30 years – he is long-suffering! Apart from that he is my second-best friend, my counsellor and motivator. Breakfast with Watto is a highlight for me. Recharged. This book is so topical it's amazing. I cannot keep from making comparisons of Watto to Saint Paul's missional approach and epistles. Watto! Keep doing the work of the Kingdom. Jim Bryant

Something very powerful takes place inside us as we glean from the hard yards of an overcomer and make it our own. Liz Howland

Inspiring, insightful, a must read for anyone who wants to have better relationships with friends, family and especially your spouse. Taken from two lifetimes of experience: Watto and Margaret. Gold! Gold! Gold! Helena Gale

I've known Watto for 30 years and been married to my wife for 21 of those years. This latest "lecture" from Ian is just what I needed to rejuvenate and reinvigorate our marriage. The memories he shares are honest, thought provoking and full of life lessons. His advice is easy to apply because these are his real feelings and real thoughts; from a real life that has been lived. Russell Modlin

CHAMPION BLOKES LEARN TO LOVE

Fifteen years ago I helped kick off Shed Nights for blokes – not the Sheds where men work with their hands but a different type of Shed that goes like this...

It starts off with a ripper burger at 6:30pm in a safe non-judgemental place where men can hear real-deep gut issues – good, bad, happy or sad – through two or three blokes being interviewed up front. It's held on the first Monday of each month and up to 150 blokes from all walks of life enjoy being together.

Shed Happens as blokes encourage each other as they do the journey of life together. They are more than happy to tell it as it is from the heart, so that others can be helped. Shed is a place where blokes are champions for who they are – not for what they do or what they have. No-one is allowed to preach, but only to tell their own story.

I go to many different places in Australia helping blokes get their Sheds happening. So that's why my book contains references to Shed and the freedom that blokes experience in their emotions, heads, souls and spirits, through being in a safe place to spill their guts and become the real deal.

Thanks!

To the girl of my dreams, Margaret, for loving into my heart and helping me write this journey.

To our three champion sons, Haydn, Brendan and Luke – for bringing joy into our lives.

To my champion editor Belinda Pollard who had to think like Watto again.

To all you champions in my life and in my Shed.

To the Champion of champions for breathing love and life into me.

CONTENTS

Howdy, champion! 1

1. Real-deal dinky-di love 5

2. Love hearts win! 30

3. Getting to the heart of real-deal love with
the girl of your dreams 53

4. How to have a champion chat with
the girl of your dreams 86

5. Champion chats come from the heart 116

6. Building a champion team with the girl of your dreams .. 146

7. Personality is not character 166

8. Learn patience 185

9. Encourage each other 216

Share the joy! 240

Howdy, champion!

How's your journey – the journey of being a bloke? Are you cruising along, or in a battle? Are you on cruise control, or had to drop down a gear to tackle a bit of heavy going?

I haven't come across a bloke who misses out on the battle. It just has a different name, time and place.

But I've never seen a bloke go backwards with encouragement. So be encouraged to know that you're OK and the battle is winnable.

When you hit a bump in the road you don't need to lose it. You'll be able to steer your way through the obstacles, and you can use it to make you better and not bitter.

The big word

Mate, welcome to one of the most talked about, most wanted, most yearned for, but – in too many cases – most stuffed-up topic. **'LOVE' is such a big word it deserves more than four letters.**

I reckon what I've learned from loving Margaret – the girl of my dreams for 54 years – helps me pass on to you some real gold, to help you take 'no love' to real love, and good love to great love.

Fellas, I'm calling Margaret 'the girl of my dreams' throughout my book. I'm steering clear of terms such as the wife, my partner, my woman, my girl or sheila, the missus, the cheese and kisses, or my lady.

Whatever stage you're at with the girl of your dreams – whether still looking for her, in a long-term marriage or somewhere in between – just jump aboard and don't get lost in any little diversions. There is stuff here to help you make real-deal love.

Another point I want to make clear from the beginning is that sexual intimacy is the Wow! Pow! of real-deal dinky-di love. Good and great sex in marriage is very healthy because it's what the Creator of the universe wants for you. If you're married and your sex life isn't healthy – then why not? Down the track, unhealthy or unloving sex, or the lack of good and great sex, can spell trouble in your marriage. So let's sort it out.

The world over, love is the thing we blokes all want – the real-deal, dinky-di stuff, not the pretend love.

So, Champion, let's have a bit of fun along the way, learning to receive love and give love more freely from deep within. It's worth it.

To get the total love package happening and flowing, I've got a few 'add-ons' in this book. They go hand in hand

with lovin' your girl, but add extra to other parts of life as well.

One of them is: What makes you and the girl of your dreams tick? It's a vital add-on that helps you understand all the people you do day-to-day life with.

Another absolute bobby dazzler is how to have beautiful and great talks with your loved one. This also helps with other people in your everyday life. When everyone who has a conversation with you feels 'safe', it brings out the gold.

And Champions, I'll also encourage you and show you how to become more patient. This helps us blokes keep love flowing smoothly – it's a must-have.

Wrap all these beauties together and man, you'll be a satisfied bloke in a great place. It's possible to kickstart love again, if you want to.

The battles along the way will never rock the inner part of you. You will be peaceful, encouraged, satisfied and joyful in real-deal love – and you can kick goals!

> Love conquers all!
> The real-deal dinky-di stuff never fails.
> Enjoy this journey with me and remember:
> Keep being you, you're OK.
> Keep amazing.

Love

It's like sunshine
in the morning
and early morning dew,
sweet birdsong
on the riverbank
like skies of
endless blue.
It's a sunset on the western plains,
a 3-hour fireworks display.
It's that miracle each morning,
the beginning of each day.

By 'Riverbank' Frank, one of my champion Shed mates.

   It's possums living in the rivergum,
      sulphur-crested cockatoos.
     It's kookaburras and galahs.
         It's even kangaroos.
    It's worth more than all the gold
         in every wedding ring.
    It's the pinnacle of human kindness,
         that sweet elusive thing.

            At its best it's unconditional,
                  sacred and pure.
               It'll lift you higher than
            the wedgetail can ever soar.
                  It isn't synthetic.
            It's not something made by man.
                  I believe it's part
               of a brilliant masterplan
            from the Creator of the universe,
               the Big Fella up above.
            It's a gift for all humanity.
            It's the capacity to love.

1. Real-deal dinky-di love

TO GET YOU STARTED

So, Champion, how are things going in your life? How's your love life? Is it good, bad, happy or sad? Are you kicking goals, or feeling frustrated or lonely?

What I have for you can take your love relationship to a new and exciting level from wherever it is now. Let's get started!

Fellas, I want to pass on to you a few nuggets of gold I've learned from lovin' Margaret, the girl of my dreams – the things that have worked for us and the things that haven't – over more than 50 years of marriage.

If Margaret and I hadn't worked through the lumps and bumps, this book of gold couldn't have been written.

You can work through the lumps and bumps too, and get the real-deal gold in your love life. We all want love and in most cases we are willing to fight for it, but we've never been sure how to fight.

Fellas, marriage is for MEN, not BOYS. Let me show you how to fight for real-deal love!

Mate, if you've been burned by love and you're thinking, 'Is this going to help me to love again?' the answer is yes! Hang in there with me and make it happen.

A romantic weekend away?

At the 22-year mark of our marriage, when Margaret was 42 and I was 43, our friends told us about a Marriage Encounter Weekend that had been a winner for them. **We didn't have any big dramas in our relationship so I thought this would be a waste of time for us, but Margaret was keen to go.**

I didn't really want to attend and felt a bit pressured on all sides. But our friends had already paid for us to go and I thought I may as well get it over and done with. So I stepped up to the plate and went.

I also thought a freebie weekend of luxury loving with my darling sounded good. **How wrong I was! It was very different from what I had in mind.**

On arrival on the Friday night my bag was checked. I had to hand in my footy magazine, form guide, transistor radio (needed to listen to the race results and scores – no mobile phones back then), and my watch. In exchange, I was given a writing pad and a biro. Wow! What was I in for?

How to talk, and how to listen

The weekend was all about learning how to talk to each other and to listen to Margaret's feelings. Yes – feelings! Learning not to just talk about a problem, but how to actually express our deep feelings about the problem with each other.

> Amazing!
> We learned how to trust each other from the deepest part within us
> and that **feelings are feelings**
> – they are neither right nor wrong.

Experienced leaders explained the process of writing our answers to their questions. They shared stories about their lives as examples for us.

We were given time to write a letter to each other expressing only our feelings on the topics given.

A bell rang and **we exchanged books, read each other's letters, and proceeded to learn some amazing things about each other.** I soon learned that I didn't know everything about how Margaret felt on some issues.

We learned that both of us had the same basic needs – to be loved, to have self-worth, a sense of belonging and the freedom to be ourselves. Problems and issues might stay the same but we learned **not to spend too much time focusing on the problem, but instead to listen to how the other felt about the problem. Yes! Feelings!**

I learned that Margaret was very intelligent and had a mind of her own. **She didn't need me to be trying to fix or solve everything. She didn't need me to be trying to read her mind – just to ask her how she felt about things and listen**. 'Love, how do you feel about this issue?' Then listen, listen, listen.

We accepted the challenge of learning to listen, not trying to manipulate each other's answers. Learning not to butt in and try to justify our opinions. Learning to have courage to hear what you may not like to hear, but need to hear.

I also learned that I hadn't got it right on some big issues because I thought I knew her so well. But I now know that you can't get into someone else's mind.

It was worth every moment for our future. We got the gold.

What we learned that weekend still stands strong with us today.

Margaret and I have been able to work pretty well through this business of going into deeper layers of issues as they come up. We've just got on better and better as we persevered and tried not to revert to old ways, or let our emotions get in the road.

Looking for love in today's world

One day recently, Margaret and I packed the X-Trail and headed south on a 2-week getaway for a bit of quality time together. Yes, we still need that at this stage of our marriage! We were going to have some catch-up rest while I put the finishing touches on my previous book.

It was about 8 o'clock on a Saturday night when we pulled into a suburban hotel/motel in Newcastle. We'd expected to drive up to the door of our motel room and check in for a quiet night – but we had to enter through the hotel.

Obviously, **this was the place to be on a Saturday night! It was throbbing with blokes and girls of all ages hanging out for LOVE. Probably, some blokes were there for the first time, others for the second or third or who knows how many times.**

We found 2 vacant seats in the corner in the crowded dining room and had a bite to eat. The women were all looking their beautiful best and smelling super. There was plenty of body showing; top and bottom. The blokes were also spruced up and the local band was about to thump. LOVE WAS IN THE AIR.

A woman staggered out from the Sportsman's Bar, sat on a nearby step and apologised to us that she was a little bit tiddly. She said that her mother would be ashamed of her if she could see her in her drunken state.

I sat back and thought, '**Here we are, with groups of women and men of different ages, shapes and sizes, all done up like fancy dress balls hoping by the end of the night to meet someone to love and just hoping that someone will love them.**' And this happens night after night all over our country.

How many blokes are still aching to be loved but don't understand the difference between love and lust?

Fellas, by the end of my book you'll know real-deal love and be able to have a red-hot crack at it.

After talking with thousands of blokes, **my 'survey' shows that blokes just want to love and be loved by a woman.** So, let's follow the old KISS principle and keep it simple. Let's give this our best shot and learn how to make it happen.

> Yes, Champion,
>   deep down inside his heart,
> man wants to love a woman.
>   Yes, love! Dinky-di love.
>
> I didn't say lust a woman,
>   I said *love* a woman.
> And guess what?
> That's what the girls want also
>   – to be loved by a real-deal bloke.
>   They want our hearts.

Love – that's what we all want. So, does it just happen? I say no, but I hope to help you make it happen from here on. If you're thinking that you've already stuffed it, hold on; we're going to sort it out!

My story

Champions, it's been 54 years since Margaret caught my eye in love and romance, when I was just a schoolboy. If you asked me now, 'How's your love life been over that time? Would you do it all over again?' I'd say,

> 'Would I do it again? For sure mate! And yes! Our 54 years of love has been overall fantastic.'

Christmas Eve 2016 was our 50th wedding anniversary, so I reckon we've stood the test of time, made a lot of mistakes, and learned enough to pass on some little beauties that aren't taught at school. These gems should not be hidden, but shared with all blokes to help change our world for the better.

Would I make any changes? Yes! I wish some tips had been passed on to me when I was in my 20s so I'd have been able to appreciate Margaret in a much more loving way.

The 50 years of marriage, learning to live with and love each other without taking a class, has been great – and we both thought we were going OK most of the time. But if I knew then what I know now, it could have been more exciting for both of us.

In my previous books, I wrote about painful issues – sexual interference at a young age, and big griefs. If they had been sorted out sooner, **Margaret would have married a bloke a bit less muddled up about love. Our love life would have been better over a longer time – open and free, early in the piece.**

Even if the love part of your life is in a mess now, hang in there Champion, it's winnable!

Where it all begins

I've found that most of the time it's the little things that make a difference in a marriage. But when no-one gives us any helpful tips, we blokes learn from and react to what we see and experience in the home and community in which we grow up. In lots of cases, we are exposed to painful and undeserved things in childhood that influence us as well.

I used to train horses (pacers), and we'd look at the pedigree to predict what a horse would be like. Well, fellas, us blokes would also do well to have a look at our pedigree. What was your sire like? What was your dam like? It's in your 'jeans'!

Champion, what sort of home did you grow up in? Sometimes we've been shown a good example, but because of stuff that's happening to us, we don't see it and learn the best things from it.

We don't have to live in the past, but lots of times, past things need to be dealt with – like I had to do. We can learn from those things. If it doesn't kill us, then we may come to a day when we can make something good out of it.

Sometimes we have been shown a bad example, and we need to learn a new way of doing things.

And if you're looking at the girl who lights up your heart maybe the same questions should be asked of her so you can sort this out before you get too far down the love road. What sort of home did she grow up in?

Have a good think about the examples you are both following. Then you can keep your guard up against potential problems, so you won't be derailed.

My 'pedigree'

When I was a boy, I saw how Dad loved my mother very much. He was a great example for me, showing her love and affection and speaking with loving words. My memory is filled with good things about their relationship. So far, so good!

But my mum died when I was 15, and everything changed for me. I found Mum dead on the laundry floor, killed by an electrical fault in the washing machine. I was an emotional mess, with stress and trauma from grief. I needed big healing that I didn't get for many years.

My widowed father worked very hard to provide for his 4 children. Two years after Mum died, Dad married a widowed lady from up the road. We all had a family again – 2 parents and 6 children – but I felt like Dad was abandoning us.

Looking back now, I know that he gave it his all and did his best, but at the time I built up resentment and bitterness towards my father. My stepmother had a hard job, because I wanted nothing less than my mother. I made judgement after judgement based on my grief and my broken heart.

I had a big chip on my shoulder but I didn't know it. I had plenty of reasons to be like that because I was in deep pain and I didn't know what to do about it.

On top of that, at a young age I was subjected to sexual interference by a supposedly trusted person. He was a church attender, like me! I wasn't able to speak out about it at that time of my life, so my family didn't know about it and couldn't do anything to fix it.

Fellas, I was in deep pain. I went around getting other people to tell me how wonderful I was and how life was so unfair to me. I was too busy thinking about my own smashed and mixed-up heart to learn how to love by the example of my home or my father's marriage.

Margaret's 'pedigree'

Margaret says...

I grew up as the eldest of 4 girls. I took on the role of the 'responsible one', and that role has continued throughout my life in many ways.

My mother was, and still is at 91, a stoic person. My father, with his fun-loving ways, balanced out their relationship. My grandparents lived each side of our home so I grew up influenced by different expressions of love and care in our mini-community of relatives and neighbours coming and going.

My faith in God was strong from quite an early age, along with my sense of responsibility and desire to obey God. I see in reflection that at that stage of my life I was quite secure in who I was.

At the end of primary school my formal education also ended. I was enrolled in a Business College to prepare me for office work (which I didn't want to do). I loved school and wanted to be a teacher but that wasn't to be. It was a miserable time for me because I'd lost contact with my friends. They had gone on to high school, whereas I began my first job at 14 and a half.

Then, at just over 15, my life took a turn for the better. I met Ian at a youth group Hawaiian night. He charmed me with his exuberance and storytelling. I'd never met anyone like that before!

We began dating and went to the Sandgate picture theatre every Saturday night until Ian bought a car and we were able to go to other places.

Ian was struggling a lot emotionally when I first met him, and although I was secure in God for him, I had my own issues of inferiority. Ian was just the right person to pour words of affirmation over me. So from the start we met each other's needs, but some years down the track each of us had our deepest needs met in Jesus.

On my 16th birthday, he said to me, 'Let's get married someday.' I wasn't ready for this! I knew I had a lot of growing up to do. I was going to evening college to try to get a better job. I had also been thinking of becoming a nurse when I turned 17.

To answer the question of marriage was serious so I needed God's viewpoint on this.

I had in my mind to marry a Christian, with blonde hair! Ian believed that God existed, but he didn't have relationship with him – and his hair was black. So I prayed and God's voice inside me said, 'He's the one.'

Well, that settled it! Eventually, I did get a better job. Then began the patient wait to get married.

I was ready by 18. Ian hadn't changed his mind, but he was quite fearful of taking that step. We were married a month after his 21st birthday and I was just 20.

What we learn as boys affects how we behave to the women of our dreams

Growing up, I dominated my 3 sisters with my know-all attitude. One of my sisters was very quiet so she hardly ever got a look-in. My older sister tried to battle with me to get a word in and she was pretty good at it too. The youngest just had to fit in somehow.

It was a bit like a lot of fruit in the blender. Everyone in the mix trying to blend together and hoping the finished taste is beautiful.

I can't remember ever thinking about my emotions growing up – that was all foreign to me.

> In our early years,
>   if we don't learn to talk about
>   how we feel,
> we can still be acting like children
>   as adults.
> That can end up being
>   very damaging to our relationships.

The consequences could be that we tiptoe around issues trying to keep out of each other's way. It's as though we're walking on eggshells just hoping for the best and that things may work out somehow.

My mother gave me lovey-dovey 'mother-smother love', and so did my grandmother. I loved every bit of it. My dad was more directional. He gave me tough love, trying to man me up and give me a bit of spine. I thought he didn't love me, even though he did.

A year after Mum died, I met Margaret. Because she was female, I expected her to give me the sooky love I was missing. I suppose I expected her to make up for the loss of this from my mother.

I dumped more onto Margaret than just learning to love each other, and it wasn't healthy. I didn't intentionally set out to do it. We can impose these things on the ones we love to our detriment.

Boys learn how to respect and love women from men, not women. Growing up, I had plenty of good and strong men around me. I could have watched how they treated their wives and the women in their lives – but I didn't take hold of their ways and learn how to treat Margaret in our marriage.

Because of things that had happened, **I had built up rocks around my heart so no-one could get in**.

But then I read this: 'I will give you a new heart and put a new spirit in you; I will remove from you your heart of stone and give you a heart of flesh' (Ezekiel 36:26 NIV). And that actually happened for me.

That little gem is from my favourite book, the Bible, which has so much practical advice for blokes that I call it the *Work Manual for the Champion Life*. (Try to get a chance to read it sometime – even if you only read bits of it. You might be surprised how good it is, like I was!)

Champion, if you're wanting a new heart, it can happen for you, too.

A story from a bloke I met in the Shed

For many years I guess I took my wife for granted. This probably goes back to how I saw my father relate, or rather not relate, to my mother.

(Check out this story from a champion mate.)

There were issues in my childhood home that I just couldn't seem to overcome. My childhood was a dark place of physical and sexual abuse, violence and despair. I even thought of ending it. Many times I prayed to a God I didn't know for it to end.

I entered my teen years with one desire: To get away and live my life my way, no boundaries that I didn't set. I couldn't trust other people. I had some girlfriends during these years – none real successful. My comprehension on how to relate to them was confused and self-centred.

So I grew up and became a man, fell in love and tried to settle down. We were doomed from the start. Her hobbies were listed as sex, sex and more sex. She came from a similar background to me – a broken and dysfunctional family, removed by community services, raised in foster care and abused by those who were supposed to care for her.

I was 27 years old when we split, and she was pregnant. She knocked on my door, handed me my baby son and left. I set about raising a child on my own with the help of my mum.

In all honesty, I didn't want any kids. I thought that if I didn't have kids I couldn't do to them what my dad had done to me. Unless you have been there you will probably never fully understand what I mean by that, but the thought of becoming my dad in how I raised my kids scared the hell out of me.

A few years later, I met my new partner. We struggled through 11 years of ups and downs. I was a present-absentee dad. I did nothing for them except cook food. I was afraid of being my father so much that I went the other way and left everything to her.

My relationship with my wife was based on the examples I had as a child. My own parents were a disaster. My grandparents were mean, argumentative alcoholics, vicious in thought and deed. My other grandparents had no contact with any of us from when we were very young.

Then we found a spiritual family which helped me to become the man and husband I am now. We met a young pastor who had kids the same age as ours. He started to teach me how to be a dad to my kids and a husband to my wife. Now we really knew who we were deep inside. We knew each other's fears and dreams.

It was hard to trust myself and there were mistakes – many, many mistakes. I loved my wife so much it hurt but I had to learn how to show it – not through jealousy and possessiveness. I had to trust her – not easy after my first child's mother continually cheating on me. I had to be open and listen to her – really listen. I had to hear her – not just what *I* wanted to hear, but what **she** wanted me to hear.

Maybe you were lucky and had a fantastic family as a child, or if you were unlucky it was like mine or possibly worse (I pray not). These things – our parents, our upbringing, our development in social circles, and our relationship with God, will all effect our entire lives. They will affect our relationships with our kids and our spouses.

When I finally started to get it

I reckon there's no such thing as luck, flukes or chances. It's destiny.

Like this Shed bloke, it was the example of other blokes that finally started to make me think there might be another way for me and Margaret. I was in my mid-30s when two blokes and their wives came into our lives. I now reckon the Big Fella – the Creator of the universe – brought them to us, but you can make up your own mind about that, Champion!

Their examples were gold for us. The way these blokes treated their women has stuck with me to this day. **I was drawn to them. I watched and listened to how beautifully they spoke to their wives. Their tone was gentle. I saw how much these blokes cared about, honoured and cherished their wives.**

Let me tell you a few little things about these champions.

George was a retired ambulance man who lived in the next street. He was a real man's man, a champion bloke. He could fix anything, change that difficult washer, and always had flowers blooming in their garden. George could talk about the Broncos and the Lions, and on fishing trips he could bait you up and tell you where to cast out and land that big tailor.

He was the same bloke whether he was speaking to the Prime Minister or giving a cuppa to the bloke living under the bridge. He was never too busy to put the billy on and listen to anyone who needed a chat. George knew who he was and Whose he was and **he showed me how to get to know the Creator of the universe on a first name basis.** I'll catch up with George in heaven someday.

Ted was our pastor for 9 years and became my mate. He and his wonderful wife lived a few doors down the hill. He showed me this special love that he had in his heart from the Big Fella for his wife. He also taught me gold nuggets from the *Work Manual* in a way that was just right for me to do my life.

He taught me about my spiritual life and showed me how to open up my heart and soul to receive the Big Fella's love so that I could love Margaret God's way. Ted is still around today and he's just the same loving encourager every time we meet or have a chat on the phone.

See how fantastic these men have been for me? If you watch and listen to someone long and hard enough, you'll soon catch the gold.

So, fellas, see how important it is to be in good company? If that's what you need **the Big Fella will give you some blokes to help you along your journey of learning to love.** Ask him to send you some, and see what happens.

> **There are plenty of top quality blokes**
> **who know real love**
> **and will encourage you along the way.**
>
> **As you're reading this you may realise that**
> **you**
> **are one of these top quality champions.**
> **Look around.**
> **There's sure to be some younger blokes in your life**
> **who may welcome your encouragement**
> **into how to love that special girl in their life.**
> **Don't hold back!**
> **Give 'em a hand.**

George and Ted had the spiritual heart dimension in their relationship with their women. This was all new to me and I wanted what they had.

For 10 years, Margaret and I did daily life with both these couples. We had the best of the best to look at, listen to and learn from about this beautiful part of loving.

This way has stuck like glue and has brought us through the bumps and lumps to show us total freedom. That could only come when we took aboard that same spiritual bit in our marriage. **It also stood us firm when we needed to heal inner pain from the past.**

There are countless things that can get in the road of real love, but your love for each other can get better and better, stronger and stronger. I've learned to love Margaret so much and I still thank the Big Fella for putting those two couples in our lives at the crucial time of our marriage. Gold! Gold! Gold!

When it's the right time I hope you can cotton on to couples like we did. Keep your radar up!

It's worth repeating this: boys learn to love and respect women from men – not from women. Plenty of boys have dads but what they all need is fathers. So if you've missed out learning this as a boy for some reason, it's never too late. Get alongside another great bloke who knows how to love and respect women and he will help you catch up.

Fellas, we can all learn to love or love again – you've just gotta wanna make it happen!

Champion blokes learn to love themselves

Champion, do you love YOURSELF? It's a bit hard to love someone else if you're always bashing yourself or putting yourself down. In my earlier years I probably had the other problem: I loved myself too much. Well, that's what I was constantly told. 'Ian, you love yourself, you're up yourself.'

> It's hard to live if we aren't loved,
> but **the Big Fella loves us**
> **and he wants us to love ourselves.**

Take care if you are bashing yourself with thoughts of negative self-esteem or even worse, self-hatred. If you see yourself as inadequate or inferior it's time you stopped believing the lie.

You're OK and you don't need to say to yourself, 'Nobody loves me. I'm unlovable.'

The Big Fella didn't make junk and His boy Jesus told us to love your neighbour as you love yourselves, and He meant it. So, Champion, if He has forgiven us for all our sins and washed us clean, what right do we have not to forgive ourselves? Enough's enough!

He gave us 100% of himself. He gives us his full love, all the time. Let's stop bashing ourselves and hand over to Him 100% of the lie so He can take care of it. Let's get on with the real-deal love. Set the spiritual part behind you loose – that's how you get real-deal love.

The Big Fella reckons the most important thing is LOVE. But real-deal love is spiritual – we can't just turn it on or off by ourselves.

If you're having trouble loving yourself, best you call out to Him to ask him to fix your heart. He can do it, and you're up and running to love the girl of your dreams.

Real-deal love is hard work

Love doesn't just fall out of the sky.
Both men and women have to work at it.

It's worth it. No pain, no gain. Whenever anything turns out great, you look back and see that you had to give it your best and work ya guts out to make it happen. That's what Margaret and I choose to do.

> If you reckon you can fall in love,
>   can you then fall out of love?
>   It was never about falling in or out
>   for Margaret and me.
> Well we did fall in love
> but it's been an act of our   will,
>   souls
>   and hearts
> to stay married and in love.
> **DIVORCE HAS NEVER BEEN AN OPTION.**

Champions, a word of wisdom that Margaret's mother gave her about marriage: 'You've made your bed, now lie in it.' Hard words, but I think that was fairly common advice back then!

You are the maker or breaker of your love.

I found that the only way to freedom was to have a red-hot crack at a heart job by the Big Fella for a clean-and-clear open relationship. Sometimes it takes a new heart or just getting rid of some of the rocks around your heart to do the job, and that's from the Big Fella. He's the only one who can do it.

Remember this gem from the *Work Manual*: 'I will give you a new heart and put a new spirit in you; I will remove from you your heart of stone and give you a heart of flesh' (Ezekiel 36:26

NIV). He will complete the job without stitches. It worked for me! Spend a little longer on this one because if you are a young gun champion it can save you heaps of pain in your future.

I hope you can get plenty out of my book to help you win through the different battles to reach real-deal love. Then when you cop a curve ball you'll know whether to hit it out of the ground or let it go through to the keeper. It will have you loving the girl of your dreams like crazy – the real-deal dinky-di stuff, the stuff that never fails.

Mate, you've gotta walk with her, before you dance with her.

TO REMEMBER...

Your feelings are neither right nor wrong.

Understanding other people's feelings solves problems quickly.

Have you worked out the difference between love and lust?

What's ya love pedigree look like? It affects things, and so does your woman's pedigree.

Women want a man's love, not a boy's. Let's step up!

If you don't love yourself it's hard to love someone else.

Joy moments

Fellas, real-deal dinky-di love brings us joy – which is not the same as happiness. These are some stories from a few of my mates around the country. Hope you enjoy them and from now on you are encouraged to write down the joy moments in your heart.

KEN: *I don't think I knew joy when I had it – wife, family, great job and health. Since my stroke I now look at doing what I am capable of, with enthusiasm and to the very best of my ability.*

NOEL: *Joy is God's stabiliser when sh*t is going down.*

GEOFFREY: *It can be meeting with the natural world or playing music with my son-in-law while his little boy dances.*

PETER: *The feeling you get by seeing the other person in your life really happy.*

DAVID: *Spending intimate time with my wife. Being with men who are open and honest enough to share their soul with other blokes.*

MICHAEL: *That unshakeable sense of happiness and contentment no matter what is going on in your life.*

ALLAN: *On the birth of our child, I knew for the first time what real joy and real unconditional love meant. Having my own family, a loving wife and my own home still fills me with joy.*

2. Love hearts win!

TO GET YOU STARTED

Champions, in learning to love the girl of your dreams, checking out your heart with the Big Heart Specialist is a must. So let's get it sorted.

How is your heart? Is it cosy and loved and satisfied? Has it been broken and smashed? Have you had a talk to it lately, or have you got it tucked away from all harm? Do you always rely on your head to solve things?

Don't move until you've had a red-hot look at your heart. Fellas, this is the heart and soul of the champion life and real-deal dinky-di love.

Your heart, believe it or not, is where the real you emerges from. If we close off our hearts, speaking only from our thinking, and lacking emotion and feeling, we can come across as dull, boring, cold or mechanical.

Real-deal love doesn't get a chance, and your girl misses out.

By looking at our hearts, we can begin a new and exciting future together.

If you had to describe your own heart in one word other than 'OK', what would it be?
Warm,
satisfied,   joyful,
   content,   cherished,   appreciated,
         broken,
            bleeding,
         bruised,   strong,
guarded,   giving,
      open,   cold,
   hard,   shattered,   empty,
            full,   romantic,
trusting,   imprisoned,
         cheated,   small,
            big,   mistrusting,
   happy,   jealous,
                     a heart of stone?

If you draw **a line representing your life at different ages, you can form an interesting picture of your heart** and how it's been treated throughout your life. Write the positive love things in all areas of life above the line and the negative things below the line, at the age they happened. Let's consider a few challenges, deserved and undeserved, that we may have encountered on our life's journey that can have huge consequences on our real-deal love outcome and how it may play out when loving the girl of our dreams.

The heart of a boy

Consider your heart when you were a baby and as a young child.

Did your parents want and love you and respond to your needs so that you kept your heart open? Did you grow up with lots of love and affection?

Or perhaps you were left to cry unattended, or sent to boarding school when young to toughen up, and you have feelings of rejection.

There are many situations in our young lives that can cause us to turn off our feelings and emotions, like constant yelling, or sexual abuse. The result is guarded hearts. We lock them away at a young age so we won't be hurt any more. We say, 'I'm not gonna cop this again.' Hearts can start to harden very early. We can build rocky walls around them for protection. This could also have happened in your girl's heart as she was growing up.

Rocks around a bloke's heart

I grew up with a sad, smashed and grief-stricken heart, **after finding my mother dead on the floor with the washing machine on top of her. I can still see it now.** She was blue and the machine was still going.

At the time, we were living in Mt Isa in outback Queensland. I had a good life there, but this event changed everything in a moment. Three days later, we were on a plane back to Brisbane. I didn't even have a chance to say, 'See you later', to my friends.

Everyone was worried about my father. No-one ever came to me and said, 'Ian, how are you?'

Back in Brisbane, I used to sit up the front at school, in line with the teacher's desk where not even the teacher could see my face. I would sit there and cry without tears. The whole year I was in absolute agony and no-one noticed.

> **I tried to protect myself from any further hits**
> **by closing up my heart,**
> **so no more pain could be added**
> **to what I was hiding within.**

Through my life after that, I always overreacted to death and funerals. One day in my 40s, it all came to a head. I was having a meltdown about the unfairness of a young woman's death. A group of close friends who loved and cared about me found me sitting at the table being miserable. They asked me, 'What's the problem?'

I told them the terrible pictures I had in my head about the day my mother died, of her hand stuck on the side of the washing machine by the electrical current. **They challenged me to replace that memory with a picture of my mother's hand in the hand of God.**

They sat and prayed hard with me about it. I didn't feel anything at that moment, but later I realised that there had been healing. It had helped remove the rocks – huge boulders – around my heart.

I've continued to live keeping my heart open from that day. My heart was opened up for the new world, and I can smile now with a free heart. My Creator kept that promise to me in the *Work Manual*: '**I will give you a new heart and put a new spirit in you; I will remove from you your heart of stone and give you a heart of flesh**' (Ezekiel 36:26 NIV).

I keep repeating it because this promise is for you, too. The Big Fella will remove the rocks from around your heart and replace it with a new heart, with the characteristics of Jesus the chippie – gentle, peaceful, kind, open and warm.

Can you believe that? A new heart! This has changed my life for the better in all ways, especially in the love area with Margaret.

I'm free to take love into my heart and free to give love out of my heart.

Breaking the rocks around your heart

Imagine I'm the average bloke. My personality might be to love and give things to people. But if my heart is still all traumatised because of the pain in my early life, you can't get in. I probably don't even know that I'm like this, because man is conditioned to be tough and not to cry.

The hard and rocky heart that's come from all types of pain and shame is smashing men (and women). It's stopping men in relationships with women. Children can't get into their fathers' hearts.

Quite often now, when I send a text to my sons I say I love them, but it felt strange at first. **Men, we've lived in our heads.**

If we don't work it out in our heads, we usually don't want anything to do with it. Once you get the power of the heart behind your head, life becomes so much more, especially in real-deal love with the girl of your dreams. And if you're ready to have your spirit come to life as well, wow!

How are you going with this heart stuff?

It's not easy to jump out of our heads and into our hearts, if we've been just doing the expected blokey thing, saying, 'If it can't be reasoned in my mind then I'll ditch it.'

If this is strange and all new to you, no worries. Don't rush it. Just check it out in your own life, and see where you go. A woman wants a man's heart!

Have you ever been in a premiership team that has just won the flag, in that moment after the final siren? Can you remember a time when you won something big-time or were filled with pride about something you'd done? **When you explode with the best emotion ever, that's the heart in you! You couldn't keep it hidden inside.**

The champion heart is open

That's why this 'heart of a man' stuff is so vital. **That heartful of joy and emotion is within you, and it's best if it comes** out where required. For too many generations men have been conditioned to keep the lid on all this soft, gooey stuff – as though it's only for females!

Our hearts can be feeling smashed in one way or another because of things that happened in the past. We can even be blokes who know in our heads that God loves us, and we're acting like everything is fantastic on the outside. But we're in deep, deep pain on the inside and feel like no-one can help us.

You've heard the saying, 'he's a hard-hearted so-and-so'. That's when a man doesn't automatically open and let others in. **That man is always guarded and so it becomes automatic to close or shut off his heart to others.** It's cruel when he does this to the girl of his dreams.

He may even appear to be a 'heart' person, but he can actually hide from reality and pretend, so as to cover up his stony, rocky heart. I've always been an open-heart person, but with the gift of the gab I can control a conversation so that I don't give you an opportunity to come near my heart. I don't even know I'm doing it – even to the girl of my dreams.

At the end of the day, if you take this approach you're being robbed of the real-deal you. You're closed.

People may detect that we're not being the real deal. They won't always tell us. Sometimes they just drift away from us. When that's the woman of your dreams, that's disastrous.

But if our hearts are open and free, we easily identify with and are drawn to other open-hearted people.

If you don't really know how to be open-hearted, I've noticed that most blokes can drop their guard with babies and connect with their innocence. **I find that being around babies is so good for my heart.** Their dependency and helplessness can touch our emotions and bring us to a good place in our hearts.

> There's so much more
>   when it comes from our hearts
>   rather than just coming from our heads.
>   Our heads always have to justify the outcome, but
> with a heart connection comes
>   freedom to be a champion
>   and closer to real-deal love.

What about you, champion?

Blokes, contrary to what society has trained in us, imposed upon us, or passed down to us such as, 'toughen up princess', or 'take a spoonful of cement and toughen up', or 'big boys don't cry', **it's OK to have a red-hot look at your heart and see what hurts are in there.**

It's never too late because the girl of your dreams and others around you will benefit greatly from your new free and open heart. You won't go backwards.

Fellas, we might have been covering up our hearts for so long that we can be totally unaware of our hearts of stone. Our outer bloke remains loving, but nothing is happening in the heart department.

No man is exempt from this heart-to-heart issue. **This has been screwing up good men and relationships for too long.** We can do a complete 180° by going straight to the top. Ask the Big Fella to put his promise into you as soon as possible, and see things turn around.

Remember, what you have chained up for 20, 30 or 40 years might need to be gently and slowly peeled away, layer by layer, to reach the champion in you, so real-deal dinky-di love can flow.

Dealing with your heart involves your 'spine, body, spirit and soul'. So when you get around to dealing with your heart, it would be fairly natural not to tell anyone else – especially another bloke who has most likely has been conditioned by manhood to toughen up too.

> **You may even try
> to deny yourself the new feelings in your heart
> because you have never before
>   ventured out of your head.
>   Take it gently!
> You'll enjoy your new heart
> and so will everyone else around you,
>   especially the girl of your dreams.**

We blokes most times don't get off the merry-go-round of life or stop in the one place long enough to even hear the soft whispers from our hearts.

It takes guts and courage to let it come out.

When hearts trump heads

If you only talk to the girl of your dreams from your head you can easily crush her heart. Your words can come like a spear in her heart. But when you can talk from your heart, your head is new and you will empower her and other hearts with encouragement and life.

Hard words from the heart heal. Hard words from the head can kill people's dreams and smash their strength.

Fellas, the world – including our wives, partners, children and friends – is starved and deprived when men don't give their hearts. It's too cold! Hard hearts keep love away.

When we meet our Creator and talk to him about our hearts, we will be in touch with our spirits because we come spiritually alive. We will have more of a 'sense of right' within us when we allow God to cut the rocks from around our hearts. We can drop off some of the past stuff that hindered our progress.

Fellas, have a little bit of a think. If we keep our hearts blocked and chained up, it is hard for us to appreciate the blessings our Creator (the Big Fella) and our loved ones want for us.

If, on the other hand, we are in a good place with our hearts, we will have freedom to give out. We will be able to really appreciate and consider those who are in the tough-heart place. If we've been there before, we can speak life and

freedom into a hard, tough heart. We can get alongside them and love them into life, and this will be a great help in developing the champion within us.

You know, if we ask the Big Fella to honour his promise with the removal of the rocks from around our hearts, he won't do a bad job on our hearts. It will be better for us and those around us – never worse.

Tough times can make you better, not bitter, if you have an open heart.

Dirty sexual areas of our past like porn and sleeping around can drop off. We won't want to offend the Champion of champions who gives us the new and free heart. The new creation within us emerges.

We can look forward to real-deal love. WOW!

A rocky heart isn't 'safe', it's lonely.

You may have difficulty in making friends, let alone love, and be living just for you and no-one else – isolated. I don't think too many blokes want that.

We really don't want to lock up our hearts, but it can happen. We can shut down our hearts towards someone if we don't get our way on an important issue.

When we are married, or in a relationship with a woman, **if both man and woman have open, free and clear hearts, then we will get the wow for each other in love.** It will be heart–to-heart.

If, however, you have gone into a relationship with a locked-up heart and you only do love from your head, this chapter will be a revelation for you. It can give you a new beginning in the champion team for your relationship. Don't get too spiro (spiritual) or serious about this. Just laugh your way to new and exciting love.

Do you know how to receive love?

Fellow champions, I showered love from my heart all over Margaret. But I didn't realise that I was holding her back, not allowing her heart to come right into mine.

I sort of knew in my mind that we could be closer, but the deep pain from grief and abuse held me back for many years, until I accepted God's promise to take away all the rocks and give me the fresh heart. I didn't drop my guard in my heart even for Margaret, and I wasn't even aware of it.

Margaret didn't have any major issues to break her heart growing up, so she was pretty free. She could come towards me, but since I had this wall I'd built up because of the pain and agony, I unknowingly held back from her.

I got into my 50s and I still didn't know that I hadn't been totally open. I hadn't been healed enough in my heart, because I didn't get anyone to talk me through it and sort it out.

Margaret says...

I may not have had a broken heart but I had taken on the belief that if I didn't do things "perfectly" I was not acceptable. That kept me in the place of thinking I was never good enough. About 15 years into our marriage I came to a new understanding that God totally accepted and loved me in my imperfection. These words from the *Work Manual* are very precious to me "… he has made us accepted in the Beloved" (Ephesians 1:6 KJV). As those words replaced my wrong thinking, my heart began to learn and become fully assured of the warmth and the fullness of the love of God in Jesus. At the time I was part of a group of beautiful women – together through sharing and prayer, we helped each other to learn, change and grow.

There are many wounded 'relationship-bearers'. People are trying to have love relationships with each other, and they're innocently being smashed. This stuff is deep down in our hearts. Most of us didn't even deserve to accumulate it, but it's a fact. It's all winnable – but you've just gotta wanna!

Nothing to give, everything to receive

When I actually received love into my heart was when I had nothing to give. I was helpless in a hospital bed.

It was after my prostate removal. Normally it's 5 weeks and you're back to work, but I wasn't getting better. The next thing I remember, I woke up in the hospital after they'd removed an appendix the size of a big, furry banana! They didn't notice I had appendicitis until it nearly burst!

I was lying in the ward after the operation with 3 drips feeding drugs into me.

Here I was, the big hero, the big giver of all gifts to all my family and everybody. **But now I had to open my heart to receive. I couldn't give anything.**

For 3 days I didn't know if I was living or dying, I was that sick. Margaret was sitting there by the bed and I said, **'Gee you love me, you really love me.'**

She said, 'Of course I do, what are you talking about?'

I said, 'No, you **really** love me.' I finally got it.

I was so weak and helpless I had no resistance, no defence to keep my heart safely closed. I'd had this beautiful woman there all my life (and so often, women just wait for their men to change!). That was the moment. At 57 years of age I suddenly knew how much I loved her, and I love her now, and I love her more.

No holding us back anymore. **Margaret's heart and my heart meet all the time and it's like an unbelievable power that goes between us.** We are more in tune in all things. Is there something like this that may be holding you back from real-deal love?

Sometimes, giving is a defence

I overreacted too much when my heart was hard, and I made it all one way. My heart could give but not receive.

I was robbed and I didn't know it. Margaret's been the most wonderful, beautiful person, but there was even more once I realised how to receive from her.

Why is the world missing out on that? Because we complicate the beautiful good news of Jesus and go on with pretend love.

I didn't know about trusting the Big Fella. I'd heard lots about him, but I never really knew him. I'd never considered that he's real and alive, so I had to ask him, 'Teach me to trust you.' We go to church and we hear a lot of things, but Number 1 should be: **Love the Lord your God with all your mind and all your heart.**

We all go through life thinking, 'Toughen up, toughen up.' **But if we actually deal with the pain by giving it to Jesus instead of ignoring it, we have the opportunity to overcome.**

Are you keeping your heart hard?

Think of the times your woman has embraced you, prepared lovely meals for you, kept herself fresh and stunning for you, and given her body to you – but your hard heart has held her at bay. She's wanted to cry on your shoulder and let her defences right down for you, but she can't get in.

She wants to help you but you have held her back and not met her heart's needs, and you know it. She can't get sexually satisfied – because you can unknowingly keep her at bay with your mind-play even though you don't mean to.

Men and women can unknowingly defeat each other with closed and hard hearts, and wonder why they can't make love work.

We blokes can be imprisoned in our hearts. This is what holds so many wonderful men and boys back from being the real-deal champion they were created to be. But we don't have to live with that anymore. God's promise is a guaranteed 'get out of jail' card.

Enough's enough! **Don't be conned and starved for true, deep love and intimacy from the one who loves you, because of your locked-up ticker.**

Listen to your heart

Think about a breakdown in what was once a love relationship that started in 2 hearts. One partner makes a choice to lock down their heart, and the relationship is immediately in big trouble. Sometimes one can't take the tough and hardened heart of the other anymore, and it's soon all over.

> **Unless one partner has the heart to forgive,
> and give the other time to renew their heart,
> it will fall over.
> Help for your heart
> from the King of all hearts
> will give both your head and mind
> new hope and vision
> to get back together.**

Being on your own without spiritual help is like the **boy with the big full barrow pushing it up a steep hill. He's got a job in front of him.** If you think you can just change your mind and sort it out you'll go a long way towards 'hitting the money', but there's still that spiritual bit that you can't manipulate.

But when we use both the head and the heart, powered by an alive spirit, we have balance. Add the hands and the feet, and we're ready to serve in the Creator's world. Let's get off our bums and get moving, fellas!

Married couples: try this for a fair fight!

Let nothing get between you. Shut yourselves in the bedroom. Take all your clothes off. No knives or ropes (ha ha) and don't come out until you've sorted out your differences. (No, I haven't tried it but someone told me about it and it sounded like a good idea.)

What about you, champion?

I've had the pleasure of listening to many women tell me that now that their men have changed hearts, everything is better. How good is that?

Sit down and have a red-hot crack at your heart and the Big Fella's promise. Weigh it all up. We'd have to have rocks for brains if we wanted to keep the heart all locked tightly away. **If you're a father or a grandfather, surely you don't want to starve your children and grandchildren of all that love in your heart!**

Money cannot buy the heart investment of a grandfather into the lives of his grandchildren. And it doesn't cost money. It costs you just being you, being the real deal.

My 18-year-old grandson knows that he's OK. I call him Champion and I say, 'I love you.' He looks me in the eyes and says, 'I love you, Pop.'

The take-home message

This is not rocket science. From travelling wide and far across wonderful Australia, I see good and solid, strong-of-character men allowing their Creator to take the rocks from around their hearts. Then they see great and wonderful things happening for all concerned, especially for women and children, and champions emerging everywhere.

Nothing changes if nothing changes. Turn your frown upside down and get on with it!

TO REMEMBER

God gives you a new heart any day you ask.
If nothing changes, nothing changes.

Broken hearts can be restored. Faulty thinking can be restored.

A loving and open heart gives you freedom.

Don't hold your heart back.

Women want and deserve men's hearts.

The girl of your dreams loves all of the above and the intimate part becomes wow! pow!

Joy moments

GREGG: *Happiness comes easy – joy needs to be worked at. Joy comes from an SMS from a long-time friend, checking on you when they could be partying with a bunch of strangers.*

Fellas, what is joy meaning to you, now you've read this far?

TOM: *Joy is a sense of being OK that stays with me whether I'm kicking goals or the world is falling down around my ears.*

DARREN: *When God is Number 1 and at the centre of my life and marriage.*

AL: *Joy doesn't come from things like a new car, boat or house. Joy comes from relationship. Joy can't be manufactured. It comes from experiencing life. It comes from the heart.*

KIM: *When my wife tells me of her 'good news' no matter how small or insignificant. To have a grandchild say to me, 'Pop, lift me on to the swing!' To have someone share with you that welcome news of a health scare that they reckon is over.*

JOHN: *Joy means being able to look upwards and outwards. Joy is God putting mates and people around me that love me and truly care about me.*

Champion love stories

Max

We started dating when I was 19, and it was lust, not love, that drove me to persist when we had dramas with her family. Her parents were very strict but they allowed me to take her to church. I only went so I could spend more time with her. My persistence paid off. We got married 3 years after we first started dating.

Real-deal champion love stories from the Shed.

What should have been a fairytale soon turned into a nightmare with lots of disappointments and regret.

I came from a traditional church background, but I didn't understand how God expected me to treat a woman. I wanted to live my life my way. I knew just enough of the Bible to be dangerous. I knew that it said that the man is the head of the woman and she should obey him. I didn't bother with the rest of the verse and regularly reminded my wife that she had to do what I said.

I started a new business just prior to us getting married. I told her once we were married she would have to stay home, and cook and clean and meet my needs. That lasted 2 weeks as we didn't *have enough money for groceries, so my wife worked 3 part-time jobs.*

Eventually the business grew and my wife worked full-time in the business. This created friction between us because she didn't like me yelling at her. I told her I was the boss and she would say, 'But I am still your wife!'

After 12 years of marriage we had a son and I was working from dawn to dark 7 days a week. I was always on call so we rarely went on holidays. There were times when my wife was at the end of her rope and she took our son on a weekend away. I didn't like that, so I bought her a spa bath so she had no reason to go. Even then, we argued about the temperature of the spa bath.

I had a few God-encounters in my life but I was not living a godly life. I stopped going to church early in our marriage. My son got to an age where he told his mother, 'I don't want to go to church – Dad doesn't go.'

I made some decisions I'm not proud of, and I got to the point where I was continually racked with guilt. I decided to tell my wife. I gave my life to God first, and I actually meant it this time. God told me things would be okay but they would not be easy. The consequences of what I had done would cause a chain of events. It would take time and the grace of God for my wife to fully forgive me and trust me again. I had to woo her and earn her trust and respect.

It was a difficult 3 years. We renewed our wedding vows and I can honestly say that our marriage is better than it has ever been. Do we still argue? Yes, but God's plan and purpose for our lives is far better than our own plans. He fixed what I had wrecked but it didn't happen overnight. I learned love is a choice, not a fuzzy feeling. God took our brokenness and built something we never believed we would be involved with. He put the right people around us so we could help other people on the path of reconciliation.

Max's wife

I mistakenly thought that if I met all my husband's needs and wants he would love me the way I wanted him to. When he stopped going to church his mother took me to a church meeting and I had a God-encounter. Early the next morning I turned on the TV and a Christian program was on. What I saw and heard was the beginning of what would change all our lives.

My mother-in-law helped me through some really hard times. She mentored me in the Bible, gave me teaching tapes and books, and always prayed for us. When I started putting God first, things started changing for the better. I learned we cannot love our spouse the way we need to without God. The Bible is the blueprint for life.

3. Getting to the heart of real-deal love with the girl of your dreams

TO GET YOU STARTED

What are the things that get in the road of your real-deal love?

Mate! Did you have a good role model in learning how to love a woman?

If you can't love yourself, you can't love another!

Many blokes need spiritual healing of shame, guilt, and the inability to love themselves. To be free to have  a crack at real-deal lovin', let the Big Fella lift ya head up, as the *Work Manual* says:

God is the lifter of our heads. (Psalm 3:3, Watto Version)

A bloke can stand taller when his head is up. He oozes honour and protection. The girl of his dreams can be the 'spine' of the relationship, and he is like the protective covering around the spine.

Then the relationship is like a rotating love ball that gets stronger and stronger, larger and larger. That's how it is for Margaret and me – not because we're perfect, but because we keep working on it. And because we've asked for help from the Big Fella.

Come on mate. Get ya head up and look into her eyes.

If you have doubts about the Bloke Upstairs and don't know if he is for real, that's OK. I had doubts, too, at different times in my life. Just give this a go, and see what happens.

The *Work Manual* says God created marriage to be a good thing – man and woman working together, supporting each other. But if we keep moving the goal posts and no-one ever knows what the true meaning of marriage is, no wonder we're in disaster mode. Champion, we can turn it around.

Woman is spine, man is covering. No competition. Man and woman's hearts are open and free to give love out and take love in and become fantastic lovers forever.

A woman loves into the heart of the man of her dreams, empowering him to become her supporter and protector, and helps turn a boy into a man. A man loves into her heart so she can become the spine of their relationship. Both can get on and be who they were created to be – no restrictions – and go like a rocket together. There's no such thing as fighting for control or anyone being subservient. We can bless each other.

Team tips from the Big Fella

Champion, building a great team starts with recognising how fantastic the girl of your dreams really is. Let's not get religious or super-spiro here. Let's just have a look at the facts, and then you consider.

How's this super gem from the *Work Manual* about how wonderful a woman can be? It's a hidden treasure that tells about a woman who lives her life in awe of the Big Fella.

> An excellent wife who can find?
> She is far more precious than jewels.
> The heart of her husband trusts in her,
> and he will have no lack of gain.
> She does him good, and not harm,
> all the days of her life. (Proverbs 31:10–12 ESV)

It talks about how she does a champion job running a home and a business, and helps people in need. Her husband is honoured in the community because he's the blessed-out-of-his-socks man married to her! She should feel like a champion also.

> She opens her mouth with wisdom,
> and the teaching of kindness is on her tongue.
> She looks well to the ways of her household
> and does not eat the bread of idleness.

> Her children rise up and call her blessed;
> her husband also, and he praises her:
> 'Many women have done excellently,
> but you surpass them all.'
> Charm is deceitful, and beauty is vain,
> but a woman who fears the Lord is to be praised.
> Give her of the fruit of her hands,
> and let her works praise her in the
> gates. (Proverbs 31:26–31 ESV)

Wow! Pow! What an amazing woman!

I grew to see how this played out for George and Ted, the champion blokes who inspired me when I was a young husband. Their wives were just like this girl in the *Work Manual*, and then I realised, so is my Margaret!

But if no-one had shown me this gold nugget in the *Work Manual* I would never have known my wife, lover and best friend Margaret – top-shelf, drop-dead gorgeous, amazing woman – fits the bill as a *Work Manual* woman in my life. Fellas, this is how good it gets.

> **Champion, is your woman like this?**
> **If not,**
> > **whose fault do you think it might be?**
> > > **Do you want to turn it around?**

Have a red-hot think about these words in the *Work Manual*. The husband and children praise this woman for how amazing she is. **Do you praise your woman for the amazing**

things she does? And remember: Your children will learn how to treat their mother from you. I've never seen anyone go backwards with encouragement!

How to encourage the woman of your dreams

I read these words aloud over Margaret, inserting our names where applicable. This empowers Margaret 'cause she knows that I think she brings these qualities into our relationship. It's powerful! No-one but Margaret and I need to be there.

You could try reading them aloud over your woman. But no manipulation! Fellas, this is not about getting her to do something you want. It has to be real-deal love and respect. It's spiritual if both are prepared to give it a crack. I know it's right for Margaret and me. Hope it helps you!

Champion, I've come from far away in my idea of love to get the good guts of this. You and God can sort it out like he and I did!

What else does the *Work Manual* say about how we should treat our wives? Have a look at this:

> Husbands, love your wives, as Christ loved the church and gave himself up for her. (Ephesians 5:25 ESV)

Or, to put it another way:

> Husbands, go all out in your love for your wives, exactly as Christ did for the church – a love marked

by giving, not getting. Christ's love makes the church whole. His words evoke her beauty. Everything he does and says is designed to bring the best out of her, dressing her in dazzling white silk, radiant with holiness. And that is how husbands ought to love their wives. They're really doing themselves a favour – since they're already "one" in marriage. (Ephesians 5:25-28 The Message)

Champion, I know this works – it has for us. I hope it helps you, too. I hope you can get the *Work Manual* gold to pass on to your woman. That's what the world is crying out for – the real-deal love that never fails. Make it happen!

Maybe these little tips may encourage you to take the time to help each other with little chores, or to do those things that lessen stress and tension in your everyday life.

If you're having trouble getting any of this to work, remember to ask the Big Fella for a service check on ya ticker. You may have had a few blockages. That can be sorted out! He's the one to get it right for you without stitches.

Lessons for young Watto

Although as a young bloke I had the example of my dad and later our neighbours George and Ted, there were still some things preventing Margaret and me from getting closer in our relationship.

Margaret had started going to some women's groups at the church, and she was becoming a bit too spiro for me. **I resented that she loved the Big Fella more than she loved me.** I didn't get the part about loving God.

But I could also see that she was changing – and that the change was coming from her heart. The spiritual stuff was working, and I was on the receiving end of all this powerful love from Margaret and I didn't know how to process it.

> Although I was still annoyed with the Big Fella,
> I decided to have a talk with him.
>   I asked him if he was real for me too.
>   I asked him to prove it
>   by taking away my swearing
>   because, though I wanted to stop it, I couldn't.
> Well, he did take my swearing away
>   – and it was after that
>   I started learning a bit more about him.

Once Margaret and I were on the same wavelength, other things started happening for us that helped us get on better in our relationship.

I realise now that God entrusted me with a young spiritual woman from a great mother and father who loved her. **She never tried to push the spiritual side onto me. She loved it into me over our journey.**

In the 1960s when I was doing National Service training at Singleton, NSW, I had a few problems. I'd been talking them over with Margaret on the phone – we were engaged to be married. After one of our chats she sent me a letter, and these are some snippets from it.

Margaret says...

My Darling Ian,

Do you remember when I said this morning that you need to talk to someone, and that I didn't know who would be the best person for you to see? Well, I think you've come to the stage in your life when you really need God.

You've been putting God off for some time now, putting in his place football, surfing and anything else you can find as an excuse.

I suppose you think I think I'm an angel or saint or something really holy to be telling you this, but I'm not (as you know). I don't think I'm any better than you or anyone in God's eyes, because we all sin. You and I have the same temptations and we give in and resist to them just about the same.

But, darling, you are missing something otherwise you wouldn't be so unsettled inside. You don't know what you want, or what you want to do and the way you are going now, you'll never find out, so I think the only way you'll ever know is to ask God.

Tell him everything – your hopes, fears, wants and just pour out your troubles to him. You can be sure he will understand and you will feel wonderful after doing it. Believe me, it works.

Don't expect to know what you should do right away, even though you may know. Sometimes it takes ages, but if you are waiting for an answer from God, it's worth it because then you will know you are doing what is the very best for you....

Don't ask once, but keep asking until you receive an answer, and even then, don't stop talking to God.

Wow! What a woman! At the time, Margaret was just 19. (I was 20.)

Margaret's still the same – smooth, steadfast, always shows up and can be counted on no matter the weather. I was looking out to sea one day at Coolum Beach and it was there that I saw the rock that describes Margaret... yeah, I'm a visual bloke. She's like a smooth well-rounded rock that always shows through as the waves roll in or out, and in any seas.

Asking the Big Fella about the tough stuff

Way back in my 20s, I remember having a squibby talk to the Big Fella. I didn't have the guts to tell anyone about this conversation for a long time.

In my eyes, Margaret was always stunning, and still is to me. But when lust was confused with love I'd perve on other women, thinking that it was a normal man-thing to do. But deep down I didn't want to.

Champion, girls know when they are being perved on. Most don't appreciate it, but also know that some girls chase it.

So I asked God to sort me out on the inside so I could always see Margaret as the most beautiful girl for me, and not perve on other women.

That's what he did. From then on, I was able to look at other women and appreciate their beauty in the right way, and it's been that way ever since. Margaret is secure knowing she's the one for me.

Why was this so hard for me to talk about? Because it was the spiritual part of me. Where in my day-to-day life could I talk about this vital point about my relationship to Margaret?

Champions, I hope my little story helps your love-heart relationship. If necessary, use it and make the change happen. It's between you and the Big Fella. The girl of your dreams will certainly know and you'll both benefit greatly. You'll want to say thank you to God for sorting you out for something we can't do in our own strength.

Put a picture of your woman on your phone upfront, not your car, bikes or kids! Keep it updated with the photo she loves. Look at your girl when you look at your phone – no-one else's picture. Yes, perve on your own girl.

Don't mess it up

Champions, please consider my following comments for all in marriage and relationships.

Sexual intimacy is equally for each other. Take care not to use it as anything else other than for true love for each other.

> No keeping score,
> withholding,
> or any manipulation for gain,
> or getting square,
> or playing games.
> > You could be sipping your own poison,
> > like a time bomb waiting to explode.
> The consequences can be damaging in a relationship.

I strongly suggest you seek very caring, experienced counsel if you've been playing with fire. You can sort it out to get the wow back. Champions, make it happen! It's worth it. Intimacy is not a thing or a toy, or something to be used to gain favour. It's a part of your whole being and it's at its utmost when it's spiritual.

I know you want the best in your intimacy. Don't mess it up. Your quality time in bed together and its beauty and amazement builds from the smallest things. Once you appreciate each other's preferences and needs, don't waste important minutes doing things that don't count.

Fellas, this is a mighty important point. Don't try **to motivate your woman into doing things for you with criticism, a dose of guilt or by throwing a hissy fit.**

If you feel that you are being criticised, bossed around, bullied or abused, just be open and honest. Gently tell your woman that you feel criticised and discouraged.

Take care how and when you do this, because you could send her into silence or yelling from anger without trying, or you could be unknowingly doing the same thing to her.

However, if you're both on the ball and you both want the best for your love relationship you'll laugh, keep on track and sort it out. But if there's only one of you on the ball, be very gentle. Tell your story with love and care and at the best time of the day. It may take time for the other person to feel safe enough to hear and understand.

A Watto Tip: Margaret and I put a good effort into making our bedroom special with colour, decorations, lighting, candles and an inviting, comfortable bed. The recent addition of an air-conditioner has been a bonus.

As nice as those things are, the real issue is what goes on in our brains. I had never thought that God would be interested in our sexual lives until the wife of our pastor gave me a book on intimacy in marriage. The author suggested inviting the Holy Spirit into our bed! I thought, "What a way out idea, but then, why not? Sex was all God's idea anyway." I was well along the head-to-heart journey so the next step was for me to give my body, my humanness to God. So I gave it a try and welcomed him into our intimacy. What a difference! But of course he was there all the time – I just wasn't aware. Give it a try.

Keeping minds and hearts open

Keep conversations about work out of the bedroom and away from the dinner table. It's absolutely great if you can find another place to do the download about work so that when you're ready to eat together or go to bed, your minds and hearts are open. **Your bedroom is for love, and rest for your soul.**

If there's tension at the end of the day because you've blown it in any way – and most blokes have many times – you can do something about it. It's important to say you're sorry. You've probably heard this said before: 'Do not let the sun go down on your anger.' It comes from the *Work Manual* (Ephesians 4:26).

If you need a big change in the way you're doing things, you can't get inside your own heart and make a change. If you want to go the spiritual way, just have a red-hot talk to the Big Fella.

Ask him to do a job on your heart, to give you the heart the one you love is waiting for. **She'll know when you change and she won't resist. She'll know before you tell her.** That's how God made women.

Only the Creator of the universe can do that, when you choose to let him in. Then you'll find that learning to love is not about you making hard work of it. The music will **come from within your heart and soul.**

I can tell you for sure it has been super gold for us over the years. Just switch onto it, mate! And be fair dinkum, 'cause everyone gets the gold as a result.

The lovin' gets better and better and you can know that the best is yet to come for many more years. But if you're not ready to have a look at the spiritual part of you, that's OK. It's your call. Nothing changes if nothing changes.

Just think how many relationships could have been saved and blossomed if we blokes had been taught more about the gold of real-deal love, way back. You'd have better known how to make the girl you love feel special and appreciated.

Here's a saying we used in footy and it also applies as you get down the track in your marriage.

> Fellas, let your performance do the talking.
> Don't tell 'em, show 'em with your actions and heart.

It's never too late. You're never too old to learn. The gold is there for those who have the courage or guts to go out and seek it. Winners are grinners!

Getting the gold of real-deal love

Remember this gem from the *Work Manual*: 'Love is of God' (1 John 4:7 KJV). The Big Fella's love never fails. It works for me, and it can work for you. All the best, getting the gold.

The Big Fella has oodles of gold in his promises for us in his *Work Manual*. It helps give us ultimate love for each other.

It's your call. If you know of a better way to get to know what the real-deal dinky-di love in your heart is, let me know, because our world has squillions of blokes desperately ready for new hearts and real love.

I haven't heard of or read any other book that can do this. So let's make the *Work Manual* a goer in the meantime – because it works.

If you realise you need help in getting some things sorted out, you may need to get alongside someone who can help you. Get a spiritual cleanout from the inside. Once the bandage falls off, ya gotta deal with the problem.

It's freeing. **It can give you a new and clean start.**

If you're not sure about the spiritual bit in you, that's OK. Don't be pushed or rushed. The gold for your relationship is winnable whatever's going through your mind.

Here's something for you to think about. It's right at the beginning of the *Work Manual*.

> And the Lord God caused a deep sleep to fall upon Adam; and while he slept, He took one of his ribs or

a part of his side and closed up the (place with) flesh. And the rib or part of his side which the Lord God had taken from the man He built up and made into a woman, and He brought her to the man. (Genesis 2: 21–22 AMP)

Woman came from the rib of man, and man is born out of the womb of woman.

I have a little experiment for you – this is a spiritual bit from the Creator of the universe. Try this with the girl in your life and see how it shapes up with you, Champion.

Lie on your back with your woman across your chest with her heart on your heart and rib – both stark naked. Stay still – no sexual stuff (if possible).

Just experience what the heart of a woman injects into the heart of man, and vice versa. If you both open your spirits to God, it's not only heart-to-heart but spirit-to-spirit – through God's empowering Spirit. This is available to all. IT'S AMAZING!

This gives me a deeper respect for the spiritual part of life that most of us blokes were never told about. Give it a go if your girl is secure and trusts you.

I guarantee your mind will not drift away into the sewers of the soul such as porn or lustful images of someone else.

See how lust doesn't get a look in when two loving hearts are open to what the Creator of the universe offers? His love is to be shared. Love never fails – especially the love the Creator of the universe made for us.

A new start

If you've been through a messy break up and are still feeling fragile, the thought of having a crack at another love relationship may have you shaking your head and screaming, 'No! No!'

There are many champions around who have been cleared from past pain, mostly with a spiritual clean out of their hearts by the Big Fella. They are ready to love again.

These blokes are worth their weight in gold to be around. They now have a greater understanding of what real-deal dinky-di love is all about, not the pretend stuff.

But not all who are single are looking for love again.

> Some who've been through the grief and sadness
> over the loss of a loved one
> wish to remain single for the rest of their lives.
> They've made that choice,
>   so take care and be sensitive.
> What you may think are good intentions
>   trying to marry them off
> can really hurt and offend.

It's not wrong to live alone. Fellas, in social situations try to include single people as much as possible.

Remember, deep pain in your heart just goes deeper until it explodes. But the Bloke who heals and gives new hearts is the only one who does it with a money back guarantee.

It's not about a bit of good advice or some religious ritual. **This is about going straight to the only Bloke who changes hearts, the Big Fella – the Creator of the universe – the Bloke Upstairs.**

Looking back, whenever I denied the spiritual part of who I am, I was the loser. There were always consequences, usually not the nicest!

So once again, it ain't rocket science – it's relational science. I don't pass this on as a theory lesson or something I copied out of a book. It was a 'no pain, no gain' experience for me.

Do the practical lesson so you can get the gold. Don't get all super spiro. I'm not trying to make you go to church on Sunday. That's your call.

What is the secret? Real love is spiritual! Yes, spiritual!

Champions, I want to repeat this.
Real love is spiritual! Yes, spiritual! So let's keep going so I can show you why and how.

The parts of a bloke

You've probably heard it said many times that we're made up of body, mind and spirit – three-part beings. What do we really mean? What's the balance?

From my observations I see that **we spend most of the journey of life in the body and mind, but don't know what to do with the spirit**. That's how it was for me.

It's all about balance. Too much or too little of one or the other and we can see why the wheels can get a bit of a wobble up. Keep this question in the back of your mind as we roll along.

Spiritual is not weird or spooky. It's freedom. It puts sparkle and wow into every glance, smile, touch, word and passion. No-one can talk you into this part of you. If you haven't met this moment yet, I hope reading my book helps you get to the gold.

How can this happen? I'll tell you about my first prayer for our marriage.

On our wedding day I nearly blew it at the church when I knelt down for the marriage blessing only to hear some chuckling from the guests. **My best man and groomsman had painted on the soles of my new shoes 'help me' in white paint.** My grandmother and new mother-in-law seated in the front row weren't impressed.

However, God has a sense of humour and he must have seen it as my prayer. He got it and still does today whenever I ask him to help me. Ha ha.

The text Margaret chose from the *Work Manual* for our wedding ceremony was **the gold nugget, 'Love is of God' (1 John 4:7). It still stands out for me today.** Why?

1. It's so short that I can remember it!
2. It works – the God-and-love part.
3. His love never fails – that's God's love for my sexual love. **And 50 years ago I didn't have a clue about God or that he was interested in my sexual life!**

I didn't realise that the Big Fella made us for a healthy love relationship, and that if you leave him out of the bedroom it's like denying the Spirit. **The natural physical part is great, but only God gives the spiritual part, and that's the best.**

What about you, champion?

If you've never spoken about or thought about the spirit part of you, or whether God could be for real or not, don't do a runner at this moment. Just push the pause button while you get all the facts.

From my experience, a spiritual blessing on the day you exchange your wedding vows has greater positive significance when the rubber hits the road than a non-spiritual blessing does.

It goes far deeper than a few words spoken to each other looking into each other's eyes. It's much more than a bunch of flowers and some ribbon on the front of a limo.

It's when the spiritual part of a man and a woman connect – heart, soul and spirit – giving you entry into real-deal love.

If a celebrant performed your wedding ceremony, that's OK. But if you reach the point of looking at the spiritual bit, no dramas, go straight to the top at any point along the way of your journey. The Big Fella will give you his blessing into your spirits from his Spirit.

God knows your hearts. He can take you to new and open hearts for each other. He certainly won't derail your marriage.

It's your call, so don't fall for 'nothing'. Go for the top shelf.

If we've come out of a family of broken relationships and divorce, we can be carrying sad and broken memories. These undeserved hurdles can get in the way of making our love relationship work.

Sometimes both people in the marriage come from similar tough beginnings. They need amazing commitment and courage to overcome the past so that it can and does work – and that's super.

When the spiritual part of one or both in the marriage becomes open, it can have a significant effect. Hopefully we can get on with a great love-heart future. Remember, 'spiritual' is not the man-made religious ceremony stuff or sitting in a building on Sunday.

Champions, look at all angles to get the best for you and your girl's situation. It's worth fighting for.

There's plenty of great help to cover all the angles, but you've gotta wanna. If you're not teachable, you battle. If in your day-to-day life you see a couple who are greatly in love with each other, keep your eye on them and get a little of their encouragement.

Go straight to the top!

It's important not to get lost in religiosity or bureaucratic denominational stuff. You can go straight to the Bloke at the top – God.

What I mean is a relationship that is one-on-one, on a first-name basis with God, nothing between you and him. **Jesus made a way for us to have this relationship.**

The culture in which we live has an idea of love and religion that misses the gold by miles. **If the world's way of love is working, how do we account for all the broken and stuffed-up relationships? LET'S TURN THIS AROUND!**

The gold is there for you if you want it. Just ask the Big Fella from your heart.

Margaret says...

Here's a prayer if you don't have a relationship with Jesus and would like to make a start.

'Lord, I confess to you that I'm a sinner. I know that sin separates me from you. Please forgive my sins. I know that Jesus died for me on the cross and will take my sin away if I believe in him. Jesus I do believe in you. I ask you to come into my life and heart, and give me eternal life. Thank you so much for forgiving me and giving me eternal life. Amen.'

And don't forget – his love never fails. He gets it right all the time.

In my early days, my idea of love was a bit too much about me and what I got out of it. But when I chose his way for my lovin' I found that he was interested in every part of our relationship, even the physical.

Do you realise that the Big Fella is looking down on everything we do? And that includes *everything* we do – even in the dark. Yes, I'm talking about sex here.

He has seen every encounter you've had, whether it was good, bad, right or wrong. But because sex was his idea right from the beginning – 'Be fruitful and multiply' (Genesis 9:1) – he wants us to enjoy it.

So if you have some hidden exploits that need a clean-up, tell the Big Fella about it. Ask him to forgive you and give you a fresh start in your lovin'. Failure to clean up your act will come back to bite when you are trying to get lovin' right with the girl of your dreams.

Girl Talk (from Margaret)

Margaret says...

We girls are not exempt from this clean-up. So many of us have been affected by what blokes have said or done to us. Some things have been so damaging and painful and been buried so deeply within that we've forgotten about or refuse to think about them ever again.

If there's any barrier between you and your lover, it may be that some earlier experience has 'frozen' you in some way. It could seem trivial to you today with your adult mind, but major at the time if you were young.

God's plan for us is true intimacy, joy, love, vulnerability and to be able to give and receive out of a place of freedom. It's freedom from the effects of unhealthy experiences that keep us 'bound' and restricted in our ability to have beautiful closeness in a marriage. But if our thinking about sex has been twisted or perverted or if we've taken part in things we're ashamed of, God can heal and restore us.

So if your love life is not a thing of beauty, love and joy today, bring all those negative experiences from the past into the light of God and ask him to cleanse, heal, mend and renew those places in you. Forgiveness is necessary – of others and yourself – and you may need to find the right people to help you talk it out and give you the tools for tearing down the old and for building up the new. It's worth it.

Beware, love isn't lust and lust isn't love

We soon discover that real-deal love is a lot more than jumping into bed with someone. It might look the way to go in the movies, but it could turn your life into a nightmare from a sexually transmitted infection or worse! Lust can end up like a Weapon of Mass Destruction (WMD).

The way love is portrayed in our culture through books, TV shows, movies and sex shops to name a few, can be seen as yet another WMD. The high number of broken relationships is enough evidence that we're off track.

Lust eventually kills ya on the inside but real love flies you to the moon forever.

If you think love comes from the 'girlie' ads in the back section of the newspaper, or from the adult shop or internet porn star, you are going to miss the gold. Facebook can be a killer if an old flame comes after you – beware!

Sometimes we blokes think this would never happen to us – but it does. Plenty of blokes can tell their stories of being lured into the den of promises by the woman down the road only to find out that they were sold a dummy. Fellas, have a look at this, from the *Work Manual*:

> Remember this: The lips of a seductress seem sweet like honey,
> and her smooth words are like music in your ears.
> But I promise you this:
> In the end all you'll be left with is a bitter conscience.
> For the sting of your sin will pierce your soul like a sword.
> She will ruin your life, drag you down to death,
> and lead you straight to hell. (Proverbs 5:3–5 TPT)

But take heart, even the consequences of this are healable with a spiritual cleanout of your heart. Go for real love that is deep and lifegiving.

In learning the difference between love and lust there will be times when you have to turn and walk – or run – away from unhealthy lust or porn or any dodgy sex – and don't go back.

You soon come to know that lust kills you on the inside and love gives you life.

Fellas, we are the maker or breaker of our love future.

If you want that extra dimension in your sex life, don't go to the adult shop – go straight to the Big Fella. Invite him into your bed, into your romance, into your intimacy – and it will be GLORIOUS GOLD. WOW! POW!

You've just gotta ask it of him, and yes it continues to work for us today. **When both parties are open to spiritual love, your bodies are God's gift to each other without any hang-ups.**

TO REMEMBER...

Sexual intimacy is for each other and no-one else. And it's not for manipulation.

If you need to get some things sorted out, don't be afraid to ask for help.

Real love is spiritual.

Ask the Big Fella to do a job on your heart, and your woman will know when you change!

What's the secret? Real love is spiritual! Yes, spiritual!

Joy moments

DAZZA: *Joy to me was when I unconditionally surrendered my 41-year alcohol addiction to God.*

GEOFF: *Joy is a profound secure emotion found safe in the biceps of God. Family feet under the meal table with lots of laughter, concreting with my neighbour when extra hands are required, patting my adorable, oxytocin fox terrier, walking on a sunset beach with my beautiful wife of 35 years.*

CHRIS: *The first time you realised that hot girl you really like also really likes you. When you found out you were the successful applicant for that job. When you realise men you respect also respect you. When your eyes are opened and you see how much God values you.*

GARY: *Joy to me is appreciating what I have, not what I haven't.*

JONATHAN: *Joy is when my daughter comes home and surprises me with a big birthday hug and says, 'Love you, Dad!'*

DARRYL: *My 81-year-old mum was rushed to hospital. Couldn't talk or recognise anyone. Joy was going back to the hospital to find a new person, talking and smiling.*

ROD: *Joy is the hope of living your dreams even when the day-to-day things seem so hard! Joy is meaningful relationships with my children, friends and workmates. It's having the support of Shed Happens to help with healing of past hurts.*

Champion love stories

Maurice

As a teenager, my relationships were self-based. Sex was all girls were for, or that's what I thought.

More stories from champion Shed blokes.

I was the creation of my father, who I hated with every fibre of my being. When I was a child he beat me and my siblings, and worse – much, much worse. I cannot fully convey in words the terror his simply calling my name would instil. Violence was all I was taught, and it was a language I learned to speak fluently.

I lived a life of violence and futility until my late 20s. To say things changed suddenly would be wrong. I met my wife and she invested in me. I considered myself lost and worthless but she saw something more.

She was stuck with the ever-growing brood of kids and I was out with my mates having fun. This, gentlemen, is not love. It is quite the opposite. Why she didn't leave me is beyond me, but I am glad she didn't.

In my mid 30s an older man took me under his wing. He told me that I can't love others if I don't love myself. But to this he added that you can't love yourself if you hate others. He told me that I did have a Father who has always loved me – God. He was there waiting for me, wanting to heal me and make me whole.

It took a long, long time, but I changed. The hatred I felt for the man who had beat me slowly turned to pity and regret.

Once the hate was gone and the regret removed, there was an empty spot left behind. The hollowness needed to be filled – with love. It started with a seed my wife had planted which was crushed by the hate, but now the hatred was gone that seed grew and bloomed.

I cried, not the tears of a small frightened child but those of a grown man who finally understood through God that there was more to life than violence and anger, fuelled by hate.

I could become a man in my own right, not doomed to be the person my dad was. I would be the man my Father (God) had created me to be.

We cannot truly love if we harbour hate – hate of self, hate of others. The longer you harbour it the less you realise that it's there. Lonely old men are creations of the grudges they choose to keep hold of. Most can't even remember why they have the grudges, but it's all they have so they won't let go.

I have had the privilege of sharing with lots of men, and the issues are many and varied. Alcohol, drugs, physical and mental abuse, sexual abuse, rejection, bullying – the list goes on and on.

I turned to God in prayer and asked for help – he answered! I suddenly saw my actions for what they were. I was shocked how she could have put up with me for so long. I had been treating her as a subservient person, there for my convenience.

I felt like a failure. What could I do? I asked God to fix the brokenness inside me. After living a life of self-indulgence, putting others' needs before your own is a hard thing.

I wasted so many years hiding the scared little boy deep inside of me. What I needed to do was truly love another person as I was always meant to do.

I tell my boys if you are hurt, cry; if you're happy, laugh. I tell my girls that they are of worth and no man has the right to tread them down. Most of all, I tell them that God loves all of them just as they are.

I share all of me with my wife, and her with me. We talk – really talk – about everything. No walls, just love. Beyond that there is a third person in our relationship and that person is our Father God.

Love contains respect, interest, sharing, caring, giving, laughing and receiving. Without the understanding that God loved me I would not be the person I am today. Today I can say I love myself, I love my family, I love God and I am loved.

Gordon

I am eternally grateful my partner stood her ground and said she wanted to spend the rest of her life with a man that shared her faith in God. I wasn't a Christian, and this concept was something I just wasn't sure about.

Like everything else in establishing this new relationship, I thought I'd just take the information in and see how it goes. I mean, I'd spent 20 years in the army. What could Christians do to me? I was ready for anything.

So I went on this journey of seeking knowledge, to try and understand what God was all about. I did an Alpha course. That was very interesting, but not life-changing. I met and began to know some really nice people – genuinely nice.

I began to change. I began to like different things. The things I used to like, I now didn't like as much.

My relationship with my partner rose to new heights and we began discussing marriage. But I was also very aware of my history in relationships. Every day I was reminded of how delicate our relationship was.

I then became involved with Shed Happens and began to put my life and my issues in perspective. Also through my story at Shed, I have been able to help other men. Now I'm also involved with the ministry to men at our new church. Helping people is what I love doing.

Ted

When we lived in country Australia the younger men would say, 'The worst men get the best women.' There was a lot of wife bashing and unfaithful men.

I have been one of the worst men and I have THE BEST wife. After years of being an obnoxious, selfish, self-centred and unfaithful husband, my wife would not give up on me. I agreed to move to another state to start a new life.

It took a long time to re-establish her trust. I had to change. We made it slowly out of the sad past only for me to suffer depression and self-doubt 20 years later. My darling, again not giving up, sought help through real-deal blokes and Shed Happens.

I'm now the real deal. I'm in God's plan and my ticket to heaven is booked. Real joy is knowing you are His, and seeing that joy in your wife. Thank God for my wife who loved me through to victory.

4. How to have a champion chat with the girl of your dreams

TO GET YOU STARTED

How do you go with conversations with the one you love? How about conversations with your family members or mates? Are they 'safe' with you?

Or have there been times when a conversation went belly-up and ended up with someone blasting off and walking off in a bit of a huff?

Or did you go into your little hole of defence, giving them the silent treatment and shutting down?

Would you like things to be different?
They can be, Champion! Let's go!

Champion chats are vital to real-deal love!

Champion, now that we've got our hearts and heads in the right place, it's time to have that special chat with your girl. In learning to love you won't get too far without talking to the girl of your dreams!

I have some little gems that will help, guide and encourage you to make it happen without manipulation, abuse or any childish games. My book will show you how to stay on track and not lose the best out of all your chats or conversations.

> **The silent treatment doesn't win love in the long term, and neither does yelling.**

Fellas, we're going to have a serious look at this most important part of lovin' and livin' every day of your life. How we talk to each other is so important! For real-deal dinky-di love this section is a game breaker. In fact, it is a country changer because it teaches us how to handle the judgement and criticism that we've suffered so much of in the past.

It helps us to be able to turn that around and find out what really pushes the other person's button – so we can avoid pushing it! We can look forward in the future to more fair and decent conversations for real-deal love.

Champions, my book is chockablock with some down-to-earth stuff that will help you love and get on better with the girl of your dreams, your family, your mates and even people you thought you couldn't put up with.

Me and my Margaret

Let's get back to my Margaret and me. She's the most important person for me to get it right with when we have a chat together.

When I first met Margaret it was all about wow! Pow! She's a stunner, she's gorgeous – hair, looks, skin and the twinkle in her eye.

In my first book, I talked about how my dead end office job sometimes felt like it was a prison, and how I could have focused on the 'bars' of that prison cell, rather than the 'stars' I could see out the window.

Well, with Margaret I couldn't see any bars at all but saw only style and stars, and she's never lost her smile and twinkle in her eye over the last 54 years. How good is that!

For a lot of those years Margaret had to listen to me blowing my own trumpet, 'Look at me, look at me, aren't I important?' What did Margaret do? She just smiled and listened many times to the same story over and over.

Margaret says...

Ian and I were married for many years before we realised the importance of having good chats where each is heard. Ian likes talking and I prefer to be a listener and think things through, but that's not a good combination when issues need to be dealt with in the 'now'.

How did we make it through all this? I loved her like there's no tomorrow, and she loved me the same way, in the best way we knew how.

Looking back, **we now have some mighty stuff that can take you to a new and exciting love no matter what stage you're at with your woman on your love journey in your life. But you've both gotta wanna!**

How did we go from me doing all the talking and Margaret happy to stay quiet, smiling with her twinkle in her eye and always speaking beautifully when asked a question? (She has never been one to waste words or waffle on.) I'll show you how we did it in these next few chapters!

It saddens us when we're in the company of couples who belittle each other with little smart remarks without any awareness of how much damage they're doing to their love for each other. Champions, this doesn't need to happen.

Get the chats with the girl of your dreams right and real-deal love is never far away.

When conversations go wrong...

Usually, when we get lost in a conversation and it goes belly-up, we go down the drain one of two ways.

We say to ourselves, 'Poor me, I don't deserve this, I'll shut down and get back at the other person by giving them the **SILENT** treatment.' I've been on the receiving end of that treatment many times from different people. It's very frustrating being on the receiving end of that treatment, especially if you're a person who's learned to 'have it out'.

The other way we can go is into some form of **ANGER**. We raise our voice, thump the table, get red in the face, the blood pressure goes up, fold our arms, yell louder and lose it. I've also been on the giving and receiving end of that treatment many times during discussions on contentious subjects.

> You quite often find that the person who loses it has
> other big stuff on their mind
> and this blow-up moment
> is just the straw that broke the camel's back.
>
> Have the courage to ride out the storm
> and invite the blow-up person
> back into the safe place again.
> Ask the question,
>   'What's really going on here?
>   What's pushed your buttons?'

I'm sure that you, too, have experienced both silence and anger. You can be sure that one of the parties in the chat will end up in either **SILENCE or ANGER, their little old defences coming out again,** if they don't feel safe.

You may not realise it, but we can keep adding all the little angry moments up and pushing them down, down, down deep within and then one day, it all comes out when something or someone causes us to spit it. **OFTEN THIS EXPLOSION**

HAPPENS WITH THE ONES CLOSEST AND DEAREST TO US.
Let's sort this out so the one we love doesn't cop it.

> Remember you are OK
> and your ideas, opinions and your dreams
> can be welcomed into the mix
>   to bring out the gold in the conversation.
> Without them it can be pretty boring.
> The girl of your dreams needs to be able to
>   safely
> bring her ideas and opinions forward, too.
>   Wow!

We build our defences in childhood

I have some questions for you. Think about how it was **growing up in your family.**

- **Around the dinner table, when and how did you fit into the family conversation with your parents and brothers and sisters?**

- How did you learn to be in on the conversation?

- Or, when you tried to get into the chat, did you end up going quiet into yourself thinking, 'What's the use of me trying to get into the conversation because no-one listens to me and they are not interested in my opinion?' So you learned to shut up and go quiet as your safe little defence.

- Did your family make you flare up with a good touch of anger with things like, 'You don't know what you're talking about?'
- Or did words like, 'You're an idiot' cause your steamy emotions to have a blast back at them as your sure little defence mechanism?

Get it?

- **Did you go into silence or towards anger?**
- **Which defence did you unknowingly take up for your survival in your early days in your household?**

Wouldn't it have been fantastic if we all grew up learning how to make good and great conversations? It sure would have saved many an argument.

Perhaps you were an only child in your family and experienced adult conversations with your parents as a norm. Maybe your parents were good at conversation, and you had no need to develop any 'get square' weapons to survive among the other children. Maybe you grew up to be a strongly independent person content with your own company and thoughts. If the girl you love comes from a large family, there may be some adjustments required to your conversational skills.

Back to me and Margaret again. **Margaret learned to go into silence in her family whereas I learned anger outburst.** My 3 beautiful sisters loved me patiently through my dummy spitting. Perhaps I needed a brother in my life so I'd leave the girls to their own peaceful games! (Of course, both girls and boys can learn either silence or anger.)

I just thought my sisters never understood me. I know now that the problem was mine. Ha ha! I'm glad I've been able to learn to own my anger, sort it out and get on to make happy conversations happen.

A story from a champion Shed bloke

For me, love was modelled by my parents being nice to each other, but not arguing. They may have argued, but it wasn't in front of me. In hindsight, I can see that I never had any role model to demonstrate how conflict should be handled. My way of thinking was that if everyone is nice, that is a happy life. I never knew what went on behind closed doors.

When I was 22, I learned that my parents were getting a divorce. Naturally this came as a huge shock to me, because I never saw them argue.

Soon after, one of my managers said to me at a Christmas party, 'You'll never amount to anything and no woman will ever love you.' Not quite the encouragement I was hoping for!

I was married at 23, but found all of this background playing out in my marriage. Instead of confronting conflict and coming to a resolution, I'd just go quiet and wonder what to do. I was then criticised for being too reserved.

Great chats with the girl of your dreams make love more exciting!

Your survival mode never leaves you until you let it go. Even years down the track, with the pressure of day-to-day living, your childhood ways of responding can come back to bite you and muck up the one you love most: The girl of your dreams.

It's all too easy to slip back into the familiar escape that developed in us in our younger days. We don't realise that our silence (not speaking) or our anger with insults and criticism came from way back then.

Champions, here's the good news. It was the same for me and Margaret until we dealt with our old defences and refused to let them get in the road of beautiful communication and love.

Years ago, I won the nod for pre-selection in state politics. I thought, 'I can make a difference, I love people and I can solve all the problems, I can change the world.' It was also a way out of my office job that made me feel insignificant. It certainly boosted my ego!

I'll let Margaret tell you what happened next.

Margaret says...

Ian had been a member for some time and obviously the party had been impressed by his verbal skills, passion and caring nature. I was quite happy for Ian to be involved as it used up some of that seemingly inexhaustible energy he had.

When Ian told me he'd been nominated I went along with it, thinking it would go no further. Then I realised we were getting into something I hadn't given much thought to.

At a women's fundraising gathering there was much excitement from everyone about the possibility of Ian being elected – everyone except me, that is.

I envisioned Ian being out night after night as well as at weekends. He would love it, while I would be trying to manage our teenage boys without the influence and leadership of their father.

I also knew how much he'd get involved with people's problems, and then there'd be the criticisms and disappointments he'd have to handle.

Unlike Ian, I didn't think I'd cope with being a public person and having to attend lots of functions. I became very fearful of what the future could hold for us as a family.

At that time, we hadn't got to the place where we would go to God together for direction. I just mustered up the courage in my own strength to deal Ian the blow by telling him I couldn't go through with it. I felt really bad, but he felt even worse. I only had to face Ian, but he had to tell the party, and deal with the pain, embarrassment and shame of pulling out.

It was a very difficult time. We didn't talk much about it and hoped our bad feelings would just go away. But of course, they don't.

When it happened, my ego came down with a thud. Man, did I tell myself a sad, sad poor-little-me story! 'How could Margaret do this to me? How come she let me get in this deep?' I felt as though everyone wiped me like a dirty rag.

But! Looking back, leaving politics was the right and better choice. I'm glad I put Margaret Number 1 and our boys Number 2, and let the political thing go.

If I'd gone into politics, would I have had my Driver Training Centre for 28 years, my water truck business, or my Shed Happens journey of 15 years? Would I have written 3 books and been privileged to encourage so many blokes on a one-to-one basis?

All these things have made it a joy to have taken the big hit of the reality adjustment on my ego. Sometimes your Creator will need to offend your mind (head) to help you mend your heart. The Big Fella woke me up.

Sometimes in our little pride moments, he challenges us within, and we have to go deeper. Sometimes the way he does it doesn't seem smart to us.

Today, we have healed from that problem thanks to the Big Fella, and Margaret – I'd die for her. She's been the best person, and a maker of our beautiful life of love together.

Margaret says...

We've learned from experience that any undealt-with issues between us need to be brought out into the open and faced or confessed. We need to ask for, and receive, forgiveness.

It's only as we do this that we grow closer together. Barriers that are between us can be washed away by the cleansing blood of Jesus and we can be open again in our relationship with Him and each other.

We made a lot of mistakes over the years, but we didn't give up. We worked at it and learned from each other and from other people.

It's now time to pass these simple, easy winners to you. For great love, you need to have a good old yarn with the girl of your dreams. These useless tactics of silence and anger should never need to get in the road again. How good is that?

Learning to play conversation tennis

Our defences of silence or anger come out when we don't feel safe. What's the solution?

If you've ever had a go at tennis, you know what it means to have a good old rally back and forwards over the net. How many shots could you get up to in the rally?

Rallies work best when both players return the ball over the net in a manner that keeps the rally going. We get to play some nice little shots, a few relaxed backhands, a few overheads, and a few lobs and we never try to put the other bloke off.

In fact, we try to keep the rally going, keeping him on the court returning the ball. One or the other eventually wins the point but only after we've both had the best rallies backwards and forwards.

We can liken this to good conversation, because what we want out of it is to keep it going – just like the tennis rally.

We may have a few shots or hard words and are not afraid to lob one up in the air occasionally, but if we trust each other we don't want to play any shifty shots against the other person so as to knock them out of the conversation. Let's play it good and fair.

On the other hand, if you think you can ace the other person with every ball it's a pretty ordinary old game. The ball never comes back over the net. No rallies, no game, poor outcome.

Remember, CHAMPION chats are SAFE

Keep tennis in mind when you want to **have a safe conversation** – keep the ball in play. The person who you enjoy having those rallies or good conversations with will always be looking for another rally, because a fair and best outcome is achieved.

If you go out on the court with someone who just wants a slam or bash and doesn't even give you a rally, it won't last long and you probably won't want to play with them again. **There's no difference in a conversation where someone is all hoi-ty-toity, or spits the dummy. You don't want to be there**.

Sometimes the other person doesn't want to pick up the ball and hit it back to you. They just don't want to try to have a conversation.

**Don't spit it!
Have a rally with the Big Fella instead –
tell him what's happened.
You can also find a practice wall to hit –
a trusted friend or counsellor
that you can talk it through with.**

We can also look at some ways to pull those conversations back. We want to bring that person into your safe place and then you will be good to be around – especially for that special girl.

Learning how to have safe conversations at Shed Night

Shed Nights have become places where blokes are safe to spill a bit of their stuff without judgement. It has taught us to open up and speak it out without fear of being ear-bashed and told that we're idiots or that our ideas and opinions are hopeless.

It's freeing and very refreshing. For lots of blokes it can be a first-time experience where they are safe to come out of loneliness and isolation, and talk.

After experiencing the benefits of being able to have good open chats shared without judgement, we blokes are also encouraged to take this into our marriages, our families and our workplaces.

This ability to make it a safe place to speak out and have good yarns about matters that are deep down in our hearts will bring rewards in our relationships. We learn skills at Shed that we can use everywhere else as well.

We try to put into practice these two gems from the *Work Manual*:

> Confess your sins to each other and pray for each other so that you may be healed. (James 5:16 NLT)
> **Watto's version: Spill ya guts and pray for each other so you can become the real-deal bloke the Big Fella created you to be.**

> **A soft answer turns away wrath, but a harsh word stirs up anger. The tongue of the wise commends knowledge, but the mouth of fools pour out folly. (Proverbs 15:1-2 ESV)**

I can say that over time, I'm learning to keep on track. I refuse to let any other comments derail an important conversation. I've made mistakes of course, but I am committed to ensuring the other person remains confident and able to express his or her opinion without judgement.

Hope you're hearing me on this one. This is gold! Get this in your set of tools and you're on the way to striking gold in all parts of your life, especially in love.

Safe conversations at work

Fellas, these skills in having winning chats also work famously in your business deals, even with the ones you try to avoid (you may call them losers, but they're not).

Wouldn't you prefer to face all people and safely listen to and engage with them, to come through with the gold that's within that person? Those conversations you missed out on in the past can in the future become some of your best.

It gets down to just being able to quickly identify how and who you are, and then being able to pick up on how the other person ticks.

You learn to gauge that point where often in the past you would have walked away from a hot topic, or there was tension in the air, or you disagreed with a statement that was dropped on you. With this new awareness you'll be able to hold your ground and create a safe place for both parties.

Some years ago, I was upgraded from a local footy coach to a state coach. The Director of Coaching at the time saw something in my coaching at the local level and he pounded me to the higher standard.

At no time did I feel unsafe in our conversations. Though he gave me a bit of an ear-bashing he never smashed me. I knew his motives were always heart-driven and with good intent. By keeping me in a safe conversational place, even though it was heavy going, he really knew how to get the best out of me. I wanted to listen and learn everything he had to offer. No pain, no gain. It was worth it. I made a success of it.

Another time, I had an issue with a bloke on my team. Everything was rolling along great guns, but one day I over-organised a situation and our communication was severely dented, with the result that the other person didn't feel safe with me. A few days later he let blast with a 21 gun salute!

There have been plenty of times in my earlier life when I would have just wiped him, 'How dare you speak to me like that!' Fortunately, this time I could allow him to be safe and let him have a good old dump and let it all come out, even though it hurt.

I thanked him for his courage in telling me, kept my remarks as brief as possible and apologised for where he thought I'd let him down, sticking to the point and not reopening the original pain.

A few days later, he quietly and humbly apologised, and I told him I forgave him. I meant it and left it at that. No patronising.

From that day on our communication's been more precise, more respectful and more understanding. He is in a better place of being able to get on and do his work better. I've learned to be more careful in my communication – I wasn't trying to bring him down with what I said in the first place, but how he interpreted it could have destroyed a good relationship.

There was a time in this conversation where it really did look like I had lost the fight, but today I can tell you that we won the war and both parties can go ahead in leaps and bounds.

> **Fellas, we can learn to handle situations like these
> at home or at work,
> and allow the other person to be safe to come back
> and not feel   ashamed,   embarrassed,
>   belittled,   manoeuvred,
>   manipulated   or patronised.**

All these issues can be multiplied for the worse where your girl's concerned, so take care.

Safe conversations with a mate

One of my closest mates and I have been practising being safe in conversations, usually with heat and tension, for over 50 years. We've proven time and again that we never go past the safe place, because our mateship is the most important thing we want to maintain at all times.

Our differences of opinion regarding politics and footy teams open up our world to see a bigger and brighter future. We learn plenty from each other.

It's not often that people change their core beliefs – but we can certainly see the big picture with what we learn from each other if we both can listen.

...and safe conversations with the girl of your dreams!

Good news mate. **Margaret and I get on like a Rolls Royce in cruise control overdrive, and it can work for you just the same. You've just gotta wanna!**

> A long time ago
> we had inside jobs (without stitches)
> done on our hearts
> so that they could be open and free,
>   and that made all the difference to us.
> This can work for you too.
> Just go straight to the top
>   and have a serious talk to the Big Fella.

Champions, it's pretty likely in the normal course of your love relationship that there will be at least one serious blow-up in conversation – but hopefully not too many more blow-ups in the future.

Let's nail this so that is doesn't happen again. **No-one sets out to fall out in conversation with their loved one.**

The main destroyer of love conversations is how we argue. We can't talk fairly! Mud-slinging, insults and criticism or the silent treatment towards each other can take over.

This can be soul-destroying. It can send us towards anxiety, depression, loneliness, disturbed sleep and many other body, mind and spirit illnesses.

Fellas, this doesn't need to happen. We need to ensure our love conversations with the girl of our dreams build love to great and strong love. We'll show you along the way how to deal with our emotions for the better, 'cause the last thing we want is a fall-out with our lover. We want to get it going better.

And how vital is it that we teach our children to have a chat so they don't grow up feeling like idiots or second-class? I reckon this has been a greatly neglected area in the past but hopefully things are changing. I have the pleasure of watching our sons and their wives communicate as loving parents with our grandchildren. I've seen and heard how they speak with their children at their different ages and stages, teaching them how to express their opinions and so learning how to get and keep the communication going in their families.

Let the music come out of you

I've come to identify the moment or moments in conversations where I have a choice to make a call in my head. I can

At the beginning of the conversation, ask yourself what the other person wants from the chat.

keep on track and not tell myself my sad story in **SILENCE** or dump on the one I love and drag her into the 'poor-me club', or go the other way to **ANGER** (yell back louder).

No, I refuse to go into my sad story. I make the choice and call. I'm not going down that path 'cause I will miss out on the gold of this important conversation.

If I want the best conversation, it's up to me.

Just think: If I'm going to dump on Margaret, that's going to make her anxious and can knock her down emotionally. I can turn her away from me without even knowing it. That's crazy!

This is vital! Don't miss it. **Going into silence or anger is like sipping your own poison.**

It's important at the start of a conversation to have these questions in mind.

1. What do I want from this chat?
2. What do I think the other person wants out of this conversation?
3. How can we stay safe in this conversation and get the best result for both of us?

> **The Big Fella showed me that
> at any moment in conversation
> I can call upon his Spirit in my heart and soul
> to take over my mouth and motives
> and ask him to guide me back on track
> to go for the best outcome.**

It's God's call in me. As I've chosen to ask God to be the guide of my life, heart and soul, his Spirit is within me and I don't need to do this battle in my own strength. I'm his consequence and he ain't going to derail me with someone I love.

It's up to you, Champion, if you want this spiritual part for yourself. You can have it too, if you want – all you have to do is ask the Big Fella!

He'll guide us back to better outcomes. He gives me a peace and satisfaction that keeps me on track in the conversation. He picks me up, dusts me down, restores my soul and encourages me back into the battle of life again and again.

The *Work Manual* says that all things work together for good for those who love the Big Fella (Romans 8:28). That's me! It works and God's got me covered. I've learned to trust him and I try to include him in every chat.

If and when you choose to go with the spiritual part of you, you have spiritual discernment within you from God's Spirit. It's another winning promise.

Fellas, here's a gem from the *Work Manual* worth a bit of good thinking time.

> The natural person does not accept the things of the Spirit of God, for they are folly to him, and he is not able to understand them because they are spiritually discerned. The spiritual person judges all things, but is himself to be judged by no-one. (1 Corinthians 2:14–15 ESV)

> **Watto's version: If we deny the spiritual part of who we are because we think it's all hogwash, we miss God's Spirit within our spirit. Without God's Spirit we can stay in our head, thinking the same old, same old, and missing the gold. But with the Big Fella's Spirit working within our spirit and mind, we can begin to understand His ways. Then**

problems and challenges in dealing with people and situations become clearer with His insight and we can expect exciting times with winning outcomes.

Taking Shed Night home with us

So let's get back to Shed Happens for a moment where we must feel safe to speak and not feel judged. We create the safe place and space at Shed.

As blokes we can't leave this at Shed. We must take this into our homes, workplaces, and especially into our relationships with the ones closest to us. The benefits of being open and free to safely speak with and listen to the girl of our dreams takes our love into another place.

No more SILENCE or YELLING (defences) – we can now deal with the tough moments in our conversations.

> Take care though,
> if you think you can go home from Shed
> and dump a bombshell on the girl of your dreams
> from something that came out at Shed.
> What you may have acted out over 20 to 30 years
> will take more than 5 minutes of someone's opinion
> to put into practice.
>
> Check the advice you wish to take home first
> with a trusted and close friend.
> Then tread gently so your girl feels safe.

> Our families are being torn apart
> because of our inability to
>   talk fairly
>   through the tough parts.

Champions, the *Work Manual* has more good advice on this one:

> **Know this my beloved brothers:**
> **let every person be**
> **quick to hear,**
> **slow to speak,**
> **slow to anger.**
> **(James 1:19 ESV)**

Ian and Margaret's tips

In our marriage, Margaret and I have come to put into practice the following valuable tips that we hope will help you.

There will be plenty of times when you'll have to consider ways to bring the other person into the safe place of conversation.

- You may have to rephrase the point. Say it in a different way.
- You may have to say sorry for being too pushy in the conversation.
- You may have to back off.

- You may need to walk away and come back to it another day.
- You may have to recreate the picture in a more sensitive way.
- You may have to re-welcome the other person to tell you how they are hearing your point.
- You then may have to reconsider your initial approach.
- You may have to accept that the other person does not want anything out of the conversation.

If it involves someone close, you may have to just shut up and listen and not get cut up because they don't show any interest in anything that is important to you. Just continue to invest love into the other person. It will come back to you one day. We reap what we sow.

More wise words from the *Work Manual*:

> **Whoever restrains his words has knowledge,**
> **and he who has a cool spirit**
> **is a man of understanding.**
> **(Proverbs 17:27 ESV)**

Remember, this is not to be in any way manipulative. Most people will shut down if they are feeling manipulated, used or abused.

This point is worth repeating – no manipulation!

The Gold that comes from real-deal champion chats

Can you see how any of your loved ones are being smashed or shut down by poor conversations or, in lots of cases, no talkie? They think it's a waste of time trying to have a fair chat. They can't get in and they don't feel safe.

Now you can invite them back into the talk by asking them to put it another way, helping the other person to regain trust in you.

The outcome is GOLD, GOLD, GOLD.

Great chats can lead to
    healing in a relationship.
They become more real-deal loving.

Loving relationships affect others.
Starting in our homes,
one relationship at a time,
we can help change our whole nation
    from judgement and criticism
    to encouragement and empowerment!

In understanding the importance of real-deal chats and making it work in your relationships those closest to you will see the amazing transformation from smashed conversation to positive and winning results.

It's easy to extend this gold into the group discussions and team-building conversations that you may be drawn into.

You can encourage all players into the safe place and welcome them into the conversation without fear. You can help avoid dictatorial moments by some people who say, 'This is the way, if you don't like it – the highway.'

Let's face it, everyone has something to bring to the mix or the project. If we don't get them in on the discussions, we can miss the best outcome and/or the fresh ideas.

One of my favourite movies is *The Horse Whisperer*. It's about a wounded horse, crazed with fear and pain that needed heaps of patience and time before it could calm down. Then someone could get close enough to draw the horse towards its treatment and healing. The 'whisperer' needed to give this damaged horse space until trust was built. Eventually the horse came close to him and allowed him to guide it along and bring about the healing it so desperately needed. Fear needed to go.

Sometimes it's like that with people who are traumatised and fearful. We need to allow time for trust to build. This works for men and women, boys and girls, just the same. Then when they feel safe and welcome back into the communication you can go forward.

You may have thought that you lost the fight, but you can now see you can win the war.

You'll never, never know till you have-a, have-a go!

TO REMEMBER...

Ensure both parties feel safe in the conversation so best outcomes are gained.

The silent treatment doesn't win love, and neither does yelling.

We learn our defences in childhood – but we can learn a new way!

Conversation tennis – play fair! Champion chats are safe.

Are you like the Horse Whisperer or The Horse?

Joy moments

RICHY: *Joy means to me: seeing my loved ones smile, giving to those less fortunate, helping out a mate in need and knowing I've done the best I can.*

GILLY (WIFE OF ONE OF THE SHED BLOKES): *A changed husband is pure joy!*

GORDIE: *Having my heart forgiven, knowing Who I belong to and that I am OK. Joy to me is also being blessed with a beautiful wife and 2 little girls who love me no matter what, and knowing* that I am their hero. Hearing my father say he loves me for the first time in 45 years. Finding freedom from being emotionally paralysed. Understanding feelings.

JEFF: *True joy is something that I think can only come out of a relationship with the Big Fella. I know that he wastes nothing, that he invented recycling. Ever since I've known him he has been using my garbage to bring hope to others.*

GAV: *Joy is having my wife happy and knowing she is unique. Also, joy is working side by side with my son.*

LUKE: *Sometimes, in bringing up kids you feel you're yelling or disciplining more than having fun with them. But then out of nowhere the hard work comes out in this kind, loving, caring, happy kid.*

5. Champion chats come from the heart

TO GET YOU STARTED

Was your home a safe place for you to express your opinion with plenty of encouragement, laughter and good conversation between your parents? This can help you understand why stuff can come between you and the girl of your dreams.

Or was it a place where you were told to be seen and not heard, and speak only when you're spoken to?

Champions, we can fix this. Conversation skills are learnable!

All our conversations could be good and healthy if we got through the layers of nothingness to delve into the nitty gritty. Layers and layers and layers – just like an onion. You just keep peeling away.

Many of us blokes don't get past the first layer.

'G'day mate. How ya goin'?'

'OK.'

'What's happening?'

'Nothin'.'

We can just stay in the nothing zone forever. Boring, boring, boring! So let's get in close with the ones closest to us – wives, fathers, mates, children, workmates – and learn to have a fair dinkum chat with them. Don't hold back from the ones you love.

You can go a lifetime without ever having a deep and meaningful conversation with someone you care about, because one person makes all the calls and the other goes along with the decision without ever expressing an opinion. That can spell disaster in a relationship.

We can just surmise what's going on but often we're wrong. We end up with the cold shoulder or a bit of fireworks, name-calling or mud-slinging just because we've let slip some words in carelessness, haste or unintended anger. I'm sure I'm not alone in this! This can be like sipping our own poison and if it keeps going, one day we have killed a relationship with the one we love. Let's get back into gear while we are able.

We can be hurting each other because of our learned communication style without even knowing it, and that can turn out exactly the opposite of what we want. Hopefully after getting the gold from my book you can have great conversations and better love.

When champion blokes learn a new way

Maurice and his wife have worked on changing the communication style he learned as a child.

Slowly I began to realise that I didn't talk enough to my partner. I knew her story – I knew she had come from an abusive relationship. But to be honest we didn't really know each other. Not the real person.

So, we started to talk and talk and talk. We peeled the layers away. We revealed our deepest layer to each other, bared our souls to each other, took the risk and trusted each other. We started looking toward God and put our faith in him. It helped to do this with the unseen 'Counsellor' there with us. This was not quick – it took years.

Communication is a word that scares most people. It is one of the most important things there is, because words have real power over people.

As a parent, you have the opportunity to control the words that are projected into your child's life. My father didn't want me. The problem with being unwanted is that you are treated as a lesser member of the family. You feel dead inside.

I have gone to extreme lengths to keep the words placed into my kids as positive as I can. My wife and I have a banned word list. It includes words like dumb, stupid, idiot, moron, useless, dopey, imbecile, hopeless, worthless. These words have destructive power when aimed at our kids.

We have 8 kids and are proud of all of them. All we ask is that they do their best each and every day. Even when they do the wrong thing and we rouse on them, when the lecture ends and the punishment is dished out the last thing we do is encourage them and leave them with positive reinforcement of a better and brighter future, one filled with love.

Gordon found a new way too.

I had the unique opportunity of another chance with my first wife, 10 years after our divorce. In the meantime I had crashed two other relationships before coming back to the first one. Even though it seemed like a fairytale, the reality turned out to be far more difficult. But there was something there that we both wanted to pursue that wasn't there before. I think it was something called maturity.

We were very careful about ensuring that, as we grew in our relationship, we checked and double checked with each other that we talked a lot about everything, to make sure that we didn't end up with a fairytale relationship that was destined for failure again.

We worked through each of our issues, but always with the goal of looking to see how the relationship could grow stronger – not building up ammunition to then fire back against each other.

This was extremely hard, because all the issues we both had with each other 10 years before were still there. But now we were tackling these issues together, not man tackling woman. It didn't get all soppy. It was an adult journey of really understanding each other, and being mindful of each other's needs.

It meant stepping up as a man to treat her properly, to be the head (spiritual covering) of the family, which meant treating her with the respect that she deserved. It meant thinking outside of myself and thinking about her needs and desires. I had to grow up.

We approached loving each other with much more mature heads. We forced each other to talk openly and fully about every little thing that was going on for us.

On one hand, this seemed a little petty that we would talk about every little thing. On the other hand, we knew so much more about what the other person really liked and didn't like. The pettiness became less as our trust for each other grew stronger – which is still ongoing.

The heart of the problem is the problem of the heart

The *Work Manual* says, 'Out of the overflow of the heart the mouth speaks' (Luke 6:45). **It means that what hits the heart also hits the mouth.** If there's rubbish and hardness in your heart that's what's gonna come out of your lips – in bucket loads.

In the spiritual part of who I am, I've learned to ask the Big Fella to show me in my heart and mind what caused me to raise my voice, and how I need to address things.

I asked him to sort out my heart and to get rid of any of those rocky bits that have hampered me in the past. I asked him to give me a new heart to get me on the way to fresh and more loving conversations with those in my circle – especially my Number 1 – Margaret – my family and the many close people I do life with.

As we've said before, the *Work Manual* says, 'I will give you a new heart and put a new spirit in you; I will remove from you your heart of stone and give you a heart of flesh' (Ezekiel 36:26 NIV). (Yes, here it is again and it's worth repeating.)

This is the proven, winning promise I hold on to. I can assure you it works for me. I hope that helps you if and when you need to have a red-hot look at this one.

This is a must with the girl you wish to do life with in marriage. She's Number 1! If you get being able to talk and listen right – life is beautiful. **But the consequences of miscommunication with your woman can mean deep pain. So we'll get this right here and now in marriage, and take it into the other areas of your life.**

Fellas, the better the conversations we have with the girl of our dreams, the better our real-deal love.

Make this happen with the one you love. It's like icing the cake or lighting the candles.

Is it them or is it you?

I enjoy people and find it easy to have a chat with just about everyone who comes across my path. I'd even talk to

the lamp post if necessary. Ha ha! I love people and am always looking for ways to give them encouragement.

But there were a few people who really pushed my buttons and I'd want to strike back. I had to change my ways and knew that I was the only one who could do it. I had to make this happen.

My little old emotions would come to light and I certainly wasn't at the top of my game. I could even shed a tear thinking, 'Woe is me!' **When I allowed it, I was smashed by my emotions and had to learn why.**

I realised that I had a common thing that happened every time. I'd blow up and feel sorry for myself and tell myself a little sad story like, **'Ian, how dare that person say those things or treat you like this, after all you've done for them! You don't deserve that.** They should show you more respect and appreciation.'

I'd have a personal pity party and yet, the next day when that same person crossed my path they would act like nothing had happened! They didn't know that they'd cut me to the quick. Then out of my soul, heart and mind, a voice said, **'Ian, they didn't hurt you – you hurt yourself. They didn't tell you the sad story of poor you. You told the sad story to yourself.'**

'No – truly?'

'Yes – you, you, you.'

What an important moment in my life. I could take charge of this moment of emotion. I was the maker and the breaker of my emotions.

Fortunately, this was never a problem between Margaret and me, generally just a handful of people who were important to me but seemed to bring out the worst in my emotions. Because it only showed its ugly head from time to time,

I tended to let it go. But as these blow-ups continued to build little by little, I realised I needed to take hold and sort it out.

I would be having a conversation and all was going well until my little emotions got pricked. **I had to realise that I was letting my emotions take control and spoil a great chat. I could stop doing that. I had a choice. It's up to me, not the other person.**

Have you ever found yourself in this spot with someone very close to you like the girl of your dreams, a family member or close mates? **If you've been suppressing your emotions they can demand expression, and this can seem to come from nowhere.**

> Hopefully you can be first to realise this has happened,
>   and help the other person back up safely from the conversation disaster.
> The sooner you sort this out the better, and you can get on and know what
>   real-deal dinky-di love
>   with the girl of your dreams
>   really is.

I am the maker or breaker of my emotions – what about you?

One of the Big Fella's champions, Paul, said in a letter, *'Don't let the sun go down on your anger'* (Ephesians 4:26 ESV).

This is so important, especially with the girl who you'll spend the rest of your life with. **This means you gotta get it sorted out before you shut your eyes and go to sleep at night, because when you wake up the next morning it's best to have your heart free and ready to go again in love and conversation.**

There's nothing worse than having the girl of your dreams hurt, and turn her back on you. Let's sort it out!

How are your emotions? You can keep going off course in conversation until you are smashed into **SILENCE or YELLING and you don't even realise what's happening.**

Much better to put up the 'time out' sign and ask for more time to think this one through and maybe resume the subject another day. **You can invite the other person back into the safer part of the conversation with a, 'Let's not go there. That's a diversion and will get us off track and rob us of a great outcome with our conversation.'**

Man up and gently bring the other person safely back into the conversation.

How Colin changed his ways

Colin's dad taught him to go to silence when there was conflict at home.

I learned from my dad to just keep quiet when things got a bit 'hot'. Sometimes he wouldn't talk for up to 3 days.

After marrying my sweetheart, I found out how much she liked talking and that she had trouble with my silence. One night she'd had enough of this and got out of bed in a huff.

She spent some time sleeping sitting up in front of the fireplace. After a while being cold and uncomfortable, she came back to bed. She gave me a big elbow in the ribs and said, 'OK, when are you going to start talking?'

So they started talking! After that night, this couple made a plan for the future. Because they follow the Big Fella, they included him in their new strategy for communication.

First the woman prays aloud and doesn't hold back anything on her heart. The man cannot interrupt her God-prayer. Then it's the man's turn. The woman cannot interrupt his God-prayer.

After each hears the other's heart as they talk to God, they quickly sort out where they are going. This works for them, so maybe it would work for you. If you've accepted the challenge of connecting with the spiritual part of you, go for it. Give it a try!

How I changed my ways

While I was blaming the other person for my problem on those few fall-out chats, nothing changed. **Once I realised it was my doings and took control of it, it was a game changer with a super outcome.**

Since I have learned these gems of good chats I can keep on track and expect great results and not get sucked in like before. I now work at taking stock of my words and thoughts so we can keep in a safe place and space with each other, without any manipulation or hidden agenda.

Champions, you can pick up these points overnight and bit-by-bit bring them into play in every conversation to see life-changing results.

> I always thought it was the other person
> who made me get into my little emotional blast off,
> but once I realised that I couldn't change
> > the other person
> > I knew
> > > I was the one
> > > who had to change.

When that happened the other person could then come with me on the journey and be safe, and we could get down to some serious business for a winning result. Got it?

Fellas, try this for yourselves. People who previously brought out the worst in you in conversation will pick up sooner or later that you have changed for the better.

What I'm experiencing is that they're speaking differently with me now and it's so freeing and getting better all the time. Because of the change in me, the freer they are to have fun in conversation. They feel in a safer place.

One day one of them may ask me, 'How come we don't have blow-ups anymore? What's happening?' We can have a good old laugh about it!

This is an absolute ripper from the *Work Manual*: 'As iron sharpens iron so one man sharpens another' (Proverbs 27:17 NIV84). This happens in conversation or having a darn good yarn.

Unresolved issues don't stay down forever so they're going to come out sooner or later sending you in the direction of **SILENCE or ANGER. If you've wondered** where those feelings all came from, now you can smash it and get the gold.

Unsafe homes

Our society is well aware of the pain men and women are inflicting on each other, even though they once loved each other in marriage or a relationship. It's a sad reality that we are now part of the increasing statistics of domestic violence and abuse. It's crazy, sad, and wrong, but when we get to the bottom of it the deep pain and hurt is in our hearts.

Domestic violence and abuse hurts everyone – men, women and children. We all pay a sad price.

Many children live through and react to this in different ways. Unfortunately, this lifestyle was their training ground, even though they didn't deserve it. Sadly, in later relationships and marriages this monster can come back to bite us. The child of abuse often becomes an abuser or gets abused again themselves. It's as if the evil seed was planted in our young lives and bears the bad fruit of violence on us and the lives of those we are trying to love. This whole thing hurts everyone.

As a society, we are frantically trying programs to solve this sadness but it goes much deeper than that. We can try to cover up an injury but a bandage only works for a while. There can still be bleeding and infection underneath. Good advice and moral support are helpful 'bandages' – but more is needed.

The only way to true freedom is a spiritual cleanout from the inside out. Ask for help from a trusted bloke, a counsellor, a community of believers and also straight from the Big Fella. Fellas, if you are hurting or controlling your woman, or being controlled by your woman, you've gotta deal with it now – don't let the poison keep growing.

The spiritual part of the heart

There's a spiritual bit to all this for me and if you've come to this spiritual part in your life you will know where I'm coming from. **If you haven't considered your spiritual part, don't switch off, you're OK. Just hit the pause button and get all the facts, spiritual and non-spiritual. It's your call.** Wherever you are at we can tidy this up and you can look forward to great chats from this day on.

In my travels across the country I meet many who have come through to be free to love and everyone wins. Let's make it happen. Keep lovin'!

The *Work Manual* says, **'Pray without ceasing'** (1 Thessalonians 5:17). **In truckie's talk that means, 'keep tuned in with the Big Fella, 24/7'.** This is good for me because it keeps my heart open and free to love out and love in, to encourage, and not to judge or criticise. That's the big one. Give up the right to get even with anyone.

> Fellas, I try to make this
> a necessary part of my day-to-day,
> not just some nice soft option.
> At any moment I go for a silent prayer –
> for wisdom
> or forgiveness
> or whatever.

These skills in conversation are desperately needed in homes, workplaces, churches, schools, parliaments, everywhere – so what about it?

Let's keep at this most important area of life so that we can gain the ability to have great and fruitful conversations with others who walk away at the end saying, 'Wow, how good was that? What a great chat. Never once did I feel left out, scared, or overpowered. I always felt secure to be able to give my best input into the conversation. And we are now charging forward with the best possible ideas and solutions.'

Yes, it's very doable, bit by bit. Don't try to fix anyone else – fix yourself.

Remember inch-by-inch is a cinch, yard-by-yard is too hard! Go into every conversation expecting to learn something, and give the other person plenty of opportunity to get into the conversation or the chat or the yarn. It's no good if it's all about me. It just doesn't work that way.

Let's practise

So knowing what you know now, practise, practise, practise. Listen, listen, listen.

The *Work Manual* says: 'A man reaps what he sows' (Galatians 6:7). **Let the music flow out from within.** The telltale signs of possible derailment are there and you will quickly identify them. **Be prepared always to give up the right to get even – that's important!**

Champions, just a reminder to consider these points:

1. What do I want most out of the situation and conversation?

2. What does the other person want out of this same conversation?

3. How best can we continue to create and maintain the safe, non-judgemental place in this conversation where we can walk away at the end with the best outcomes for both of us? That's what we're after!

Those closest to you can be the most difficult because of the strong emotional connection. Fellas, take notice of this point because that's not where we usually expect the problem to be.

There may be other matters from within or without that have upset them and you're copping it for no reason and you can't understand why. **Remember, there's always more to the story.**

I'm gonna repeat this: There's always more to the story, so stand by and listen, listen, listen. Winning chats are exciting because they work. It ain't rocket science.

Champions, you are now the maker or breaker of good conversations. Make it happen!

Getting help from the Big Fella

At the start of a conversation that's likely to be difficult, if both parties are spiritual people a quick prayer to the Big Fella is the way to go. Ask for his help to guide our motives and heart through to hearing clearly and making it to the best outcomes.

This works for Margaret and me. **There's no need to get too super-spiro in this because God knows our hearts and our motives.** We can leave the consequences up to him and he can always be trusted.

I'd pray something like this:

> Dear God,
> Please direct my words in a manner that you would have me say them from my heart,
> so that they can be heard the way you would want them heard by the other person.
> Thank you, Lord. Amen.

It sure helps you sleep with a clear conscience when you know you haven't blasted someone out of the ballpark. Champions, I know this works! Stay with it, you will be set for the rest of your life and you will kick goals.

Margaret and I took a bit of time to be confident to talk openly to the Big Fella together, mainly because **I wasn't confident that I knew him well enough. I had to overcome that by asking him to teach me to trust him. It's easy for me to chat with him now.**

I'm glad I sorted that out 'cause Margaret and I can go for it with the Big Fella on any issue now, and that's GOLD. The 3 of us have some good laughs from time to time. Hope you too can have a crack at this, but it's your call.

This is another of my favourite gems from the *Work Manual*: **'God's ways are bigger and better than ours'** (Isaiah 55:8-9 Watto Version) – so go get great and better conversations that make it so good to love, love, love.

Good and great conversations bring out the best in all situations!

Difficult conversations

Champions, sometimes the conversation doesn't go anywhere or can be difficult. Be aware that you or the other person in the conversation:

- can have a hidden agenda
- don't and won't LISTEN, or are only tokenly listening

- are shy or scared of saying something wrong
- are the 'I'm not good enough, poor me' people
- want the other person's guts, but then want to do a runner
- are the arrogant know it all
- are the perfectionist – 'look at me, look how good I do everything'
- are the emotional person who cries at the first drop of a hat
- just 'spit it' and shut down on the other person as a weapon
- tells all their stuff and never asks how the other person is
- finds fault with everything that is said
- delights in dropping big clangers on the other person
- are patronising
- belittles the other person
- says, 'I know, I know, I know.' But they don't. (Or you don't.)

If any of these are going on between you and your girl you need help ASAP.

Keep in mind that there's always more to a story and why people act like they do. Get the more! And if it's you, wake up to yourself! You now know how to have a fair conversation and get back on your game. Enjoy the conversation. You're OK!

Ask the Big Fella for help. Listen, listen, listen. Be prepared to give up the right to get even. Don't try to fix them – fix yourself… and you might be surprised how things start to change.

> I hope you can see that
> every which way you turn in life
> > there's an opportunity to have a conversation.
> If you've started life
> without a lot of help and encouragement
> to make it happen,
> you can miss out on so much fun and laughter.
>
> Let's make it happen.
> We have a choice
> > to make it or break it in conversation.

Champions, you're never too old to learn or change but you've just gotta wanna.

What comes out of our mouths can make us or break us

How many times have you put your big foot in it? Sometimes it happens before you realise what a disaster you may have caused. Just say sorry if you need to, and make sure you mean it from the bottom of your heart. It ain't over till it's over.

We certainly need these chat skills for those closest to our hearts, especially the girl of our dreams.

We also need the skills of having a great chat with our teacher, pastor, coach or boss. We also have to do life with people we see as 'pains in the neck'.

It all boils down to what you really want out of any conversation, so think about it, and know what you want. This goes for all conversations.

Fellas, Margaret knows that it's my wish never to offend her in any way because she trusts me. I hope you can build similar trust with the girl of your dreams and your chats are as sweet as honey.

Start in your heart.

- Ensure that she doesn't feel threatened or embarrassed, or that either of you need to win or lose.

- Take care in your chats not to do the old 'information download' on the other person.

- Take care not to make your story too long, and avoid trying to read her mind, just let the chat flow from your hearts.

- Sometimes you may have to take the bullet to help the other person gather strength to join in.

- Ensure the other person in the conversation doesn't feel overpowered or 'set up'.

- No manipulation.

You'll soon learn to identify those times that will make or break the chat, so be ready to change your sails for a new direction at any stage. It's worth it.

Smooth seas don't make great sailors

Smooth seas don't make great sailors so don't be afraid of some rough water from time to time. It brings out the best in you.

Smooth conversation could be covering some potentially dangerous undercurrents. So make sure you listen with your heart.

If you've been caught off guard, or feel that you're having a bomb dropped on you, or you are temporarily stumped for words and you are not ready to talk – relax, you don't have to rush.

Just say, 'I don't know the answer and I feel confused. I will try to come up with the facts but I may need time to sleep on it. I'll have to get back to you on this.' Keep your cool.

Above all else, remember you are OK.

Champion, I'm going to repeat this. You're OK!

The game is not over till it's over. You have heard this before in my book, but it needs to be taken in.

As I've already said, you can lose the fight but you can still win the war. You may need a little more thinking time.

Put the billy on and have a red-hot talk to the Big Fella. Ask him to show you his way so you can get the best results.

I've already said this too: 'His ways are always better than yours or mine' (in the *Work Manual* – Isaiah 55:8–9, Watto Version). **That's why I like to have a cuppa and a chat with him to compare his way to my way and get the winning way.**

Champion, in your work situation, these conversation skills still apply. If you feel your boss is trying to railroad you there's no need for you to go underground. You may need to have a chat about this problem with a trusted person to help you find a way into a safe place of conversation with your boss.

Also consider time, place and space before you confront the situation. Sometimes your first emotional reaction isn't always the most effective way to deal with it.

FIFO chats

Fellas, we men work hard to earn and will even fly-in-fly-out (FIFO) for the love of a woman. Flying in and out for weeks at a time can be real tough – being away from your wife, your bed, the touch and smell of the girl of your dreams.

So we need all the help we can find to get the gold and make it happen, to keep the real-deal love happening forever amidst the many battles. We may need to learn all over again how to communicate with those we love most. We've had to learn to live apart, and that can cause friction and frustration.

While my mate Barry was away at work, his wife and adult daughter got on with their lives, keeping the home fires burning without any problem. When he returned home, Barry's tone and the way he put things sent the girls into silence.

Eventually, his daughter lovingly let him know that when he came home it unsettled the flow of everything that was going along OK. Poor old Barry didn't even know that living away had toughened him up. He could have thought that his family didn't want him around anymore. Not true! They all came to the realisation that there was a readjustment needed in communication to get back on track.

So where does Barry or any other bloke go for help to change? Most times we revert to old ways that can hurt those we love. We've all had similar battles and can be a bit touchy from time to time.

> **The Big Fella gave Barry's family what they needed to get back safely into great love and conversation – plenty of love, appreciation and gratitude for each other without manipulation.**

Sometimes when we go into silence it could be about something else that puts us under the pump – money, sex, work or relationship problems, to name a few. These can consume us and when we arrive home we can 'lose it' and blast off at someone, stuffing up a good relationship.

Barry owned the problem of communication and sorted it out so he could be right with his wife and daughter. They were all prepared to speak openly and give up the right to get even or score points. Winners are grinners.

What about you, Champion?

If you find you are running into snags with 1 or 2 people you care about, you can have a look at how your emotions play out.

There's nothing wrong with your emotions. Your emotions are your emotions. Once you realise that they play out sometimes in really big ways you can address them.

You can't change the other person. I know because I had to sort this out in me big time. The other person can change as a result of the way I have changed. I can guarantee you that this has worked for me.

I asked the Big Fella for help because it's better and deeper and long lasting. I was desperate to make sure I wasn't gonna stuff up with the most important people in my life. No more emotional derails. No more pity party telling myself my 'please feel sorry for me' story.

> Keep focused and make it happen.
> Champions, this will work for you. It always works for me.
> Keep it as simple as possible. The old KISS principle!

So Champions, let's get cracking and in every case let's make great conversations so we have a win/win outcome.

Fellas, I hope you've enjoyed this journey into ensuring that you can have safe, enjoyable, meaningful and stimulating conversations – especially with the ones you love – and walk away feeling joy from being able to make it happen.

I guarantee this will change your life for the better. Margaret and I continue to grow in love for each other and having these sure winners in our conversations. We make it happen – with help from the Big Fella.

Champion chats are for life

Margaret kept an old cake tin containing love letters from the 60s and our letters from that Marriage Encounter weekend in the 80s. When this book on learning to love came to happen, Margaret pulled them out of the cupboard. Wow, how exciting! They are treasures – just to read those again makes my heart ping. Those letters remind us how much we wanted the best for each other, way back then.

From that 80s weekend to this day after 50 years of marriage, at any place, any time or any issue, Margaret and I can step aside and listen to each other's feelings and make it happen.

Yes, we could be at the MCG on Grand Final day amidst 100,000 people and just step to the side, switch onto each

other's feelings on an issue and sort it out.** This is continuing to produce the 'wow' in our love for each other.

This great advice does not go out of fashion. It still works today. So if you need to do a course like we did, if you and your girl take it seriously and keep at it you can start the change for the better happening in your relationship overnight.

No more just back and forward, discussing the problem over and over, getting nowhere. Get past it. **Make it happen. Have fun!**

I hope you can cotton on to this and apply what works for you. **Grab this sure winner. Listen to each other's feelings and sort it out.**

So how does this measure up with you? If you haven't been into listening to the feelings of the girl of your dreams and seeking to know what matters most to her each day, here's something you could try.

A great question to ask your lover is, '**What things matter most to you today, Darling?' This can be one of the most important things you will say to her each day.**

Don't rush her, and have **no agenda.** Listen hard to her answer and if necessary, jot it down and get on with trying to help her in those areas.

Don't forget to ask gently, either with a call or text through the day, or if it works better, ask the night before what's important for the next day. Do it mainly to listen, show appreciation and give encouragement.

You can teach each other how to get the best out of this. It's gold. She'll get it sooner or later and ask you what matters most for you. Then be ready 'cause the gold starts to rush.

> If you take up this challenge for 30 days
> you'll find it's worth it big time.
> Don't expect her to do the same for you.
> But if you can hang in there
> I reckon you will have well and truly got the picture.
> I'm sure you'll be pleasantly surprised
> with heaps of gold at the end
> and find that it's a big winner for both of you.

The Big Fella has shown me in my life that there's heaps more gold for us blokes. He showed me how to act in conversations with others, especially with Margaret, our 3 sons, our employees, and also the people who don't agree with my comments on politics, my denominational views or my footy team and other hot topics.

He has helped me to listen more and ensure I have greater respect for the other person and their opinion. I keep on learning to stay in conversation to get this gold. Get what I mean?

It can change a good relationship into a great love relationship.

TO REMEMBER...

We learned how to talk to people in childhood – but we can change it!

You are the maker or breaker of your own emotions.

For new and free real-deal love, you need to give up the right to get even.

Don't go to bed angry. Sort it out.

Ask for help from the Big Fella!

Joy moments

REECE: *Joy is knowing God has my back. Being content with what I have and forgiving quickly. Peace and joy seem to go hand in hand for me.*

PETE: *Knowing that this is not all there is.*

GLEN: *My wife is named Joy. Her aunt died suddenly at 18 not long before Joy was born. The baby's arrival turned great sorrow into joy. So to me the joy of the Lord overcomes the deepest sorrow.*

MICHAEL: *The joy of the Lord is a gift that refreshes me daily. It gives me great confidence in the hope for better days ahead.*

BRUCE: *Joy is that state of being alive, bringing a private smile without the need of an outside stimulus.*

PAUL: *Joy is a deep knowing that everything is going to work out and the Creator thinks you are a top bloke because he has made you.*

LARS: *My son came home absolutely wrecked and slumped on the couch. He asked me if we had any tigerbread left but it was all gone. The joy was for me to drive to Woolies and pick up Nutella, Danish butter and a fresh loaf of bread and present that to my son.*

BIRCHY: *Joy to me is in knowing God has blessed me with a fantastic family who all love Jesus, working every day on the land that God created.*

6. Building a champion team with the girl of your dreams

> ## TO GET YOU STARTED
>
> As man and woman, it's in our life together that our strengths and weaknesses show up – and our clashes. But with a better understanding of how and why each other ticks, we can *make love happen* like there's no tomorrow.
>
> So let's have a go at sorting this personality thing out.

Our world is filled with amazing people and we come in all shapes, colours and sizes, with different likes and dislikes. Together we make up the team of life. **We need other people, whether it's a partner, family members or friends. We can't do life well alone.**

Fellas, getting to appreciate each other's differences is easy and very worthwhile, so let's not make hard work of this. Keep it simple. It's been a winner for me in getting on with people, so that's why I'm passing it on to you. In this chapter we want to gain a better sense of who we are, and how it affects others around us – to make love more real-deal.

What makes you tick?

When I began teaching people to drive a truck, everything was going pretty well. It was exciting. I loved the interaction with people and especially the challenge of getting them through to their licences first go. **But there were some blokes I was having a bit of trouble with. I just couldn't seem to connect with them**. My way of trying to motivate them was frustrating for both of us.

Mr Peaceful

These blokes gave me the impression that they didn't even want to be there. They didn't talk much, and appeared to be in their own world. Compared with my exuberance and drivenness, their clock seemed to tick so slowly that at times I thought it had stopped. **I wondered if they even wanted to be in the truck with me.**

Mr Peaceful is a calm bloke and likes a life without worry or conflict. He doesn't push himself forward, show off or come across as more important than anyone else. He's a

great listener and prefers to let others do all the talking or run things, and he's good at keeping his thoughts to himself.

Margaret could see my dilemma and did some personality research to help me understand and appreciate my truck driving students better. She found something that identified 4 main personality types.

It said we all have a mixture of the 4 personalities but usually 2 of them are more noticeable. Certain ones can emerge in different situations. It really helped me, so let me tell you Personalities According to Watto! This is what I call the 4 main personalities in Aussie blokes' lingo.

> **Mr Happy Party Boy**: 'Everybody's my mate. Let's have fun!'
> **Mr Peaceful and Laidback**: 'Stay calm – no stress.'
> **Mr Attention to Detail**: 'Let's do it right.'
> **Mr Boss, Leader and Make-it-happen**: 'I'll get it done.'

Champions, how do you see yourself? Hope you can catch on without too much fuss and bother.

This helped me to accept all students and help them enjoy the training too. **Once I knew about different personalities I didn't lose customers at the end of their first lesson, and my business grew rapidly. I learned to bring out the best in others.**

If you know me you can easily understand why an hour with **Mr Peaceful** may have been pretty ordinary for both of us because at that time, I couldn't understand why people didn't do things my way. **I'm the hard driving, bossy bloke with the extra gene of emotion, feeling and passion, looking to be the life of the party.** I know now that I must have almost driven some poor blokes insane with too many instructions.

Something had to change and that had to be ME!

The type of bloke I was having trouble with in my driving school is an introvert. He's sensitive, quiet and doesn't like to be rushed. Too many words tire him and he likes to works things out for himself after minimum instructions.

Yes, you've got it, he's opposite to me!

You might recognise him as you – or as the woman of your dreams. Knowing how we all tick makes life so much better when we learn to appreciate each other's differences. It makes life exciting.

Does your personality get you into trouble from time to time and you can't understand why? Mine sure does, without me even trying.

I'm a bloke with the personality of Mr Boss and Mr Happy. Growing up, my personality caused me many a lonely tear and a slightly bruised heart. Ha ha!

Margaret reckons at times I'm still a bit too touchy with little things that hurt my heart. Yes, I'm still learning to cope with my emotions! But it's OK, that's my temperament.

If I didn't know who I am, I could flare up time and again with too much touchiness about little things, and turn people away from me. Because I now know who I am and what makes me tick, I'm not trying to be like someone else. I'm OK, and I can appreciate others who are different from me.

Clashes of personalities can create huge dramas at work, in your families, teams, clubs or churches. It happens everywhere. We need to work out how to stop it happening, especially with the girl of your dreams.

Mr Happy

I learned that without any effort or putting on an act, my personality is **Mr Happy – the entertainer.** The more people around me, the happier I become.

I have an encouraging, positive and affirming attitude towards others. People don't tire me at all but give me energy. I like to be popular and I get a little hurt when someone doesn't like me. I have lots of friends and regard all 984 contacts in my phone as my champion mates.

I like to make things happen, but I don't worry much about the middle bit of the project. I don't mind how or who does this part, just get it done! And let's try to make it a party along the way – everybody's welcome. That's me!

What matters most to people like me is having fun with others no matter what they are doing. Remember, I don't have to work at this – it just comes naturally.

If you're like me and 'out there' most of the time, you are described as an extrovert. No worries – your personality is you. Appreciate who you are.

Have a little think about others you may know who are also like that. Have you been able to enjoy their company or have they annoyed you?

Mr Boss

Another aspect of my personality shows like this. I can accept a tough challenge and at times can appear to be aggressive. I'm a 'driver', and not just of trucks! I'm a 'make it happen' man. I'm ready to solve your problem – even if you didn't ask!

The big question for this part of my personality is, 'Who's in charge? Let's make it happen.' I can come across like Mr Boss, Mr Leader, Mr Make-it-happen.

Are you like this? Maybe you can identify others in your circle of family and friends who act this way. Again, this is perfectly normal. **You're OK – don't try to be someone else.**

When Mr Boss comes out of me some people cringe if they've only known me as the party boy. They can read me the wrong way. This serious, focused, driven part of my personality may come out looking angry.

But I'm not angry. I'm just driven with dominance, passion and emotion to bring in the big guns and go for it and get the gold. I'm not trying to change you, though you may think I am.

Which combination are you? They're all good!

The way you can hurt this type of person is to show them no appreciation for their efforts. The nicest thing you can do for me is say, 'I appreciate you.' And because this type of person appears to have it all together, they can be lonely and they can be seen as not needing anything.

The truth is that everyone needs encouragement – even those who always appear to be on top of things.

Your personality will come out naturally. There are a lot of blokes out there getting unfairly smashed and criticised for just being their natural selves.

Our 3 sons are similar to us in some ways but distinctly different from each other. **All 4 personalities show up in them in different ways at different times – as would be the same in all families.**

We've always encouraged them to be themselves and try to appreciate each other's strengths and differences, and to enjoy and sometimes laugh at themselves over these differences.

Our sons are married and have children. It is important for all of us to respect each other. Learning to understand each personality has been gold so that every family member feels loved, respected and included in the wider family.

Mr Detail

Another personality type keeps us on the straight and narrow path to make it happen. He is very creative but may get lost in the journey trying to do it better, trying to be perfect.

He likes to do things his way – even though it may not be the best way. This bloke is good for me as he brings out my best and he makes me think deeper and harder. **But because of the way I do things, I can come across to this person as slack or disorganised.**

What matters most for this **Mr Detail** is to cover all bases correctly in detail. Don't we all need one of these people in our family or team to get things done well!

How does this one fit with you? It's just good to be comfortable with who you are.

Don't let this get complicated. It's as simple as saying the ABC. We need to appreciate the bloke who likes to do everything right and **we don't want to smash him by branding him a control freak**. He may want us to do it his way because he thinks it's the right way and maybe the only way, and yes, it could be the right way. He will crack up if you unjustly brand him.

However if he is a control freak he will openly smile and give you a nod of acceptance and just get on with taking control. My personality is OK with a bloke who is in control 'cause he makes it happen. I can get alongside and get on with what he wants from me in the project.

Just note this. You may think I would clash with this bloke, but because types like me are very comfortable in who we are, we can go great with a control freak. It even gets better as we work together and grow in trust with each other.

Notice I have given you a quick look at 4 personality types to show you how important it is to appreciate each of our differences. **No-one is better or worse than the other** but we can rub each other up the wrong way if we're insensitive to how our personalities show up.

You want to love a woman, but you've got to be prepared to appreciate that she's going to be different to you! If you find it hard to know what type of personality you are, there is wonderful stuff being done to help you work it out. If you want to do an online test to figure out the differences, try searching for '16 personalities' or 'life languages'. That will lead you to a couple of different questionnaires to help you figure it out. Some are free, and some you have to pay for.

At home

The more Margaret and I understood how each other ticked, the more it helped us to LOVE and accept each other and to stop thinking our own way was right. Her personality is a mix of Mrs Peaceful and Mrs Detail. Margaret really values harmonious relationships. She has lots of friends and is calm and collected (unless under pressure).

Living with me in the early years of our marriage must have been like living with a travelling circus for Margaret, but she loved me and was determined to make our marriage work. Maybe I'm still like a circus at times, just older and slower.

Margaret says...

For me, my home is my haven but for Ian it's an open door. We both grew up with lots happening in our homes and enjoyed it, but as an introvert I need some time alone to recharge my batteries. As an extreme extrovert, it's taken time for Ian to understand this and accept that

I don't have the energy he has. We've learned to balance this out somewhat in our later years – although he'd still love to socialise every day and every night of the week if he was physically able!

Even though we were and still are very different, we complement each other.

I'm sure there are many couples who don't have a clue about different personalities and wonder why they clash so often. It's **tragic and crazy to think that with some basic understanding of personality differences, they could have kept beautiful love flowing instead of going.** It doesn't have to happen.

So let's go after the gold, to understand our differences and put the knowledge into practice. You've just gotta wanna! Enjoy yourself – especially in your LOVE.

The purpose of this chapter is for you to be you, and to be very happy in accepting yourself – your strengths and your weaknesses, warts and all, and to appreciate the girl of your dreams and other blokes better.

You don't need to run away when you come across someone with a completely different personality or temperament to yours. You can stand tall.

Enjoy the difference!

Margaret is a combination of Mrs Peaceful and Mrs Detail, so she is totally opposite to me. What matters most

for Margaret is that she likes meeting people's needs and caring for them. She also values some alone time.

So how do we get on?

You often hear that opposites attract and it's been that way for us. Two people like me could never live together! Fancy having 2 of me in a marriage!

We get along like a house on fire now, but there have been times when we couldn't understand each other or get our act together. Our love for each other has kept us working through our differences. We've had years of practice. Our togetherness has gotten better and better over our 50 years.

> **A Watto Tip:** I'm not too much into detail with the middle stuff in planning a project, whereas Margaret's at her best in that area. So for our Mediterranean cruise some years ago I just said, 'You know what I like, and I don't think we'll be coming back this way, so take care of all the details. You do a great job.' And the cruise couldn't have been better. (By the way, I did say to her, 'Don't tell me how much it's going to cost.') This is how things work for us.

Doing special things for each other

Margaret and I can tell you without doubt that there are special things that we do for each other, and the way we do them makes our hearts go, 'Ping!' We feel deeply loved on the inside.

Are there things your loved one does for you that make you feel special? Have you worked out what makes the girl of your dreams feel like a princess?

The easiest way to figure it out is to see what each of you automatically do. If she's always saying encouraging things, or if she gives you little gifts, that's probably what she'd like from you.

Just roll with this mighty simple stuff that works. Work out what makes the woman of your dreams feel cherished, and do it. Try, try and try again – and if necessary say you're sorry – 'I got that wrong.' Champions, make it happen! Try again soon. You'll end up with the gold and you will love and appreciate each other heaps more.

Fellas, a little tip – this is how it works for me with Margaret.

She's a tidy girl and I'm untidy. So I know what to keep tidy around the joint – like not leaving dirty clothes on the floor and keeping the kitchen sink clean and clear. She likes the rubbish taken out to the bins.

I have one of the rooms in our unit as my 'shed', sleep-out and office. Margaret tolerates my untidiness there because she knows I'm comfortable. She understands me and regularly comes in to vacuum and dust, working around my 'mess' (as she calls it). It's all good – no problem.

See how this works? These are things I wish to do for her, and that she wishes to do for me. It makes our hearts ping and show each other more love 'cause we know we're appreciated.

We live in a unit so we have two flights of stairs. Whenever I can, I carry the groceries up from the car. When Margaret's car needs a clean, I'm the man. Ironing is not her first choice but she won't let me pay someone else to do it. However, she appreciates it when I enjoy doing some ironing while watching footy. Yes! This works for us.

Margaret's a good cook. She likes to run the kitchen her way – and that's OK with me. She spoils me with lovely meals and by the way she presents them. We both like candles so we often light a candle for our evening meal.

Some days I call Margaret around smoko between 9am and 10am and say, 'What's on tonight? I'm cooking (which means, 'I'm taking you out for dinner'). What's your taste sensation today?' Margaret doesn't have to prepare a meal and she loves my spontaneity that puts wow into our love. Try it!

> **A Watto tip:** We usually do to others what we would like them to do to us, so keep your radar up. See how you are treated, and return it. You'll get the GOLD!

Champions, this doesn't have to cost dollars. Get the old brain into gear and come up with some ideas. Once again, listen to each other's heart for clues so you can come up with some surprises. It's the little things that put the wow pow into your love. Come on, you can do it!

Here's a little note from Bill, one of the Shed blokes who finally worked out what made his wife's heart ping.

It took me years to figure out what pressed romantic buttons in my wife's brain. She is so opposite to me – as most wives are to their husbands.

For my darling, things like doing the vacuuming, cleaning the toilet or hanging out the washing were better than a movie night or romantic dinner – which we often couldn't afford anyway.

I asked her only recently, 'What makes you happy?' I felt a deal of shame when I heard her answer, 'I'm happy when you are happy.' The Lord dealt with my shame, but I had to ask her to forgive me for the times when I had made her sad or unhappy.

Like a lot of blokes I made a great choice to go to God. He has blessed us because my choice has stuck with us throughout everything. What an awesome God who loves us first and last.

You are the maker or breaker of this one. Hope you get it quickly.

Who's in charge?

You might be the stronger one at your house, and the girl of your dreams might be more gentle. Or maybe you and your loved one are the other way round, with the woman the strong one and the bloke the more gentle one in the relationship. **Gentleness doesn't mean weakness.**

If your personality mix works best for you this way, be accepting that it's perfectly OK for a woman to make the tough calls. It's equally OK for a man to be the soft and nurturing part of the relationship.

Just be aware of what matters most for each of you. Act on that each day and enjoy making real-deal love happen.

What's this got to do with better love? It may sound a bit crazy but it all gets down to working out what matters most for each person in the relationship. So I hope you can get some gold out of this.

When the power of love overrules the love of power we'll start kicking goals and getting the gold. If you want your love relationship with your girl to be great we need to give up all our power games. They just get in the way.

No more power plays in your love ... they kill!

TO REMEMBER

Mr Happy Party Boy: 'Everybody's my mate. Let's have fun!'
Mr Peaceful and Laidback: 'Stay calm – no stress.'
Mr Attention to Detail: 'Let's do it right.'
Mr Boss, Leader and Make-it-happen: 'I'll get it done.'

What's the personality type of your
girl? Accept her for who she is.

We're all different, and we're all OK.

If we work out what everyone's good at
and respect it, we kick goals.

Joy moments

TIMBO: *Joy is standing on my deck in the early morning embracing the freshness of a new day whatever it may bring. Joy is the grateful reflection at day's end, gazing at a canopy of stars that enfold my perspective of time and space. Joy is the love, encouragement, support and belief of faithful friends and family who carry and sustain me, especially through times of trial. Joy is the sense of purpose, peace, hope and the unconditional, abiding, relentless love of the One who does not change, who knows me completely and yet loves me still.*

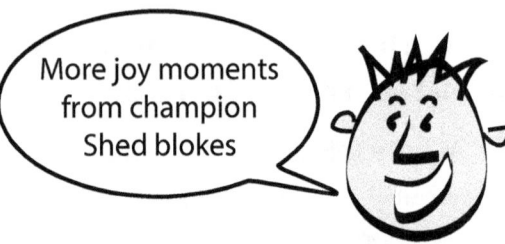

NICK: *Joy is finding the moments of peace in amongst the chaos of the day. When I'm out moving cattle with my beautiful bride and cruising on the ag bike on an amazing autumn day.*

FRED: *Joy for me is being alive in this amazing world. Being blessed with family and friends, an amazing wife, 3 great sons and their wives and 10 grandchildren all vibrant and unique, mates that are true and real.*

TINY: *Whether it's a helping hand, our time, a listening ear, or words of encouragement, joy is always received when we are giving from an honest loving heart.*

MARK: *Joy is my beautiful wife, grandchildren, a son who is still clear of cancer.*

Champion love stories

After 2 decades of marriage and 4 children, this champion couple renewed their vows. Here are some snippets from the vows they wrote for each other.

Her vows:

You have always understood the value and fragility of a woman's heart, and you have taken such precious care of mine. You have kept your promises to me, Babe, by your words and your actions. You have been faithful, loving, tender and patient.

You have always made me feel like the most important and beautiful person in the room and have shown incredible support to me, investing personally in my dreams and encouraging my passions.

You have listened to and cherished my hopes, treasured my most private thoughts and feelings, and given me a safe place to fail and to try again.

When I struggled with depression and the wheels fell off my world, you were there alongside me shouldering the burden and loving me through the craziness. When surgery made me question my worth as a woman, you made me feel more beautiful and desirable than ever.

When the strains and pressures of life have come, and I'm feeling like I'm about to break, you have been there comforting and calming me with your words and prayers. In all these moments you keep pointing me to the Father and trusting Him completely.

I love that we can laugh together, learn together and grow together. I love that you don't wait for a special occasion to buy me flowers. Loving you is so easy, and my love for you has only grown deeper and stronger since I first gave you my heart.

This time I say, 'I will' with a greater understanding of what it takes to keep the promises we made to each other all those years ago.

His vows:

These first 20 years have been an amazing journey and it has been such a privilege to share my life with you, my best friend.

I truly value you for who you are and who God has called you to be. You are incredibly wise and insightful. You always seem to know the right thing to say, at just the right time and in the right way.

I cannot thank you enough for your loyal support and devotion to me and our life together. Thank you for all the sacrifices you have made supporting me and our family.

On that day I promised to love, cherish and honour you, to be faithful to you, to care and to provide for you. Today I would like *to draw another line in the sand and publicly recommit to those promises.*

I promise to continue to see you for who you are and what God has called you to be. I will do all that I can to see you fulfilled in every area of your life.

I will always honour you, both in public and in private. I will always be faithful to you. I will always put you first and seek God for his blessing in every area of our life. We have witnessed first-hand his blessing on our marriage over this first 20 years and I am confident that he will continue to bless our life together.

7. Personality is not character

> **TO GET YOU STARTED**
>
> Do you know who you are, and you're not afraid to be different from others?
>
> Can you laugh at yourself?
>
> Can you cope when someone has a different opinion to yours?

Fellas, **don't confuse personality with character. Character is another vital part of who you are**.
It's developed in your life from things you've learned. It's affected by people you do life with and the choices you've made from your family background, your upbringing and many more things that you take into your being.

My dad, favourite footy coaches, uncles, school teachers and a neighbour 2 doors down the street who had no children of his own all added to my character development.

The difference between personality and character is that personality is what you are born with, the 'face' that everyone sees day in and day out. Character is the deep you – your core being, your spine, your integrity, your foundation.

Since acknowledging the spiritual part of me, God has been the main source of my character development. His Son, Jesus, has been helping me make right choices. You might wonder how that could work, but Champion, stick with me and I'll show you how it worked for me over the chapters to come.

Your personality may be extrovert or introvert, shy or confident, energetic or relaxed, secure or insecure, funny or sad, positive or negative and more.

Your character may be good or bad, strong or weak. Good character shows out in areas of kindness, honesty and integrity to name a few. Character shows up from the inside out. Character is what you do and who you are when no-one is looking.

Who are you when you're on your own and no-one's looking?

It matters who we spend time with

As your character is developing you can be attracted to certain people, good or bad, and they can have an effect on you. Putting yourself in good and positive company = good character. Putting yourself with low-life characters = down goes your character.

It's about choices or chances. It's important to help other people become better characters if you can, but sometimes you've just got to turn away and run from shyster living because it can drag your character down.

I really enjoy being in a group of people who are confident in knowing who they are, with their own personalities and strong character, yet who are able to appreciate each other. They respect one another's strengths and differences, with an awareness of the things that could annoy each other.

> **This is a group that doesn't shut down,
> clam up, have a hissy fit or spit the dummy
> when the conversation may introduce a little tension,
> or someone has a different opinion from theirs.
> This group can listen to the whole person in you,
> and laugh and get on with it.**

People like this are game-makers and innovators. Their creativity just oozes. They're great to be with. **It's super to be with people who can laugh at themselves.**

This is all gold and the best can come out in all of us, because we're comfortable with living on the edge and enjoying it.

If, on the other hand, people are on edge and defensive, the conversation can't flow. We're too cautious in case someone's offended. It's like walking on eggshells. This is not very exciting. It can be boring when everyone's worried about saying the wrong thing.

What do you look like and how do you come across when people are looking at you? How does your character shape up?

Champion, do people like to be with you, or would they rather give you a wide berth?

Hopefully after you get to understand yourself and accept who you are it will be easier for you to join in and enjoy being with other people.

We're all unique!

The issue of personality is and has been very important for me because growing up with my personality type was painful at times. I often felt lonely. It seemed everyone was picking on me and rubbishing me because I was 'out there' all the time and sort of in people's faces. My personality is to have a big opinion on all subjects – and that can get me into trouble.

I attended a workshop with 50 other driver trainers one day. One of the sessions was with a psychologist who guided us through a personality study. After a series of questions he posted up a huge chart with lots of boxes with different descriptive words in each.

The psychologist called all the answers and matched the people in the room with the boxes. Then he asked, 'Anyone left without a box?' and yes! It was me.

When I told him my score I was the only one to match up with the box marked 'Entertainer'. So there you are – I had to accept who I was that day and be happy to like myself – as different.

Don't be confused with who you are. You're OK and don't let anyone tell you otherwise. I don't get embarrassed by who I am anymore.

So be encouraged – be yourself and like yourself. You have much to contribute.

Understanding the differences helps us

This chapter will help you kick goals, make your relationships great, love better and better, help you succeed at work, help you and others achieve goals more easily, and bring out the best in those doing life with you.

Your personality is the outside, visible part of who you are – who you look like on the outside to others around you. Own yours and enjoy who you are.

I wish I'd known sooner about different personalities. It would have helped me understand others. When I was younger, I might have persisted longer with other people instead of writing them off, calling them 'losers' or thinking them dull and boring.

I'm telling you a lot about **my extroverted personality** not because it's the best kind, but because learning how I tick made a big difference for me. I want you to get to know just who you are because I reckon **we blokes need help with this.**

Your personality most probably won't be like mine. So don't write me off, because I'm not writing you off. Don't push the 'stop' button, just hit 'pause' every now and then and have a think.

Personality tests are great when they help us appreciate another person, but it's very important that we don't label and put each other in a box as though that's the way you are and you'll never be any different.

You may have experienced times when someone tried to put you into a box and shut the lid. Or you might have had a negative stamp or brand put on you when you were young.

That's cruel and can hold you back in your development. It can prevent you becoming the real you. It happens because they don't really understand you and it can hurt big-time.

It's not because you're no good. It's because they're seeing you through the eyes of their own personality. Those glasses they're wearing may not show them the gold in us – or how different we could become.

But if there are aspects of our personality that are offensive, these can be dealt with. Our personalities are not set in concrete. With the help of the Big Fella the positive side can shine and the negative part can be transformed.

If we allow God into our spirit we can be continually changing to become more like his Son, Jesus, who was the most perfectly balanced person that ever walked on the face of the earth.

The Creator of the universe showed me his box doesn't have lids!

This is worth spending a little time thinking about. You can break free and enjoy becoming that person that the Big Fella created you to be.

The Creator of the universe showed me that his box doesn't have lids. You can become that person he created you to be. So don't be boxed in any way, shape or fashion. Be free to flow!

When you come to know what makes you tick and also what makes those about you different, it takes away a lot of stress. It can save many arguments – without you having to lie down or give in.

Understanding personalities helps you be a better father

As a young father, before I appreciated anything about personalities, I was more about 'just do it my way', or you were yelled at. Our ponies Roughnut and Donut were pretty placid. One of our sons rode them bareback, yelling and screaming like an Indian scout. Another was not like that, but I just put him on and said, 'Get going!'

I treated him the same as his brother, and it was painful for him. The same thing happened when I was treating them to surf – the boogie board, the surf ski and surfboard.

If I'd known what I do now about personalities, I definitely would have been more understanding with the differences of our sons. It could have been much better for everyone, instead of me yelling instructions like I was back doing Army Basic Training.

We have a laugh about it now, but back then it caused pain and stress because I didn't consider each son differently.

Fellas, if you are a parent, have a very serious look at this. Understanding your personality and the personalities of your children can make a big difference.

Your personality may be Mr Detail, for example, and your son or daughter might have a bossy, leader-type personality. You may think you are helping them by talking them down, only to find out too late that you have been firing them up and making them angry or sending them into silence.

You can also drive them away and they can turn towards unsavoury things to cover their pain.

A parent with a dominant personality can send a quiet, shy, introverted child into fear. The parent may not even realise this is happening. The child can take this fear into later life and have big emotional dramas.

> **Your children may never feel appreciated for what they are naturally good at, because it doesn't fit into your box.**
> **You may be frustrating them**
> ** and none of you understands why.**
>
> **Know how we tick and it doesn't have to happen.**
> **You can sort this out –**
> ** but you've gotta wanna!**
>
> **Get to know the few main areas of their life**
> ** that are important to them.**
> **This will help you show special interest in them.**

If this is your story, say sorry and get on with explaining how you're now coming to understand how they tick, and also understanding yourself more. Then watch them go like a rocket.

Winners are grinners

Your personality isn't acquired. You don't have to try to get one! It's the natural you that arises out of your emotions and thoughts.

I'm still the same personality at 70 as I was when I felt like I was being wrongly judged as a boy (that was my take anyway, 'poor little Watto' – haha). You are who you are.

When you really know how you tick, you learn to see what's going on and how the other person in the conversation feels. You can be more sensitive and always get gold instead of mud in your face.

Don't stress. You can have some thinking time to understand where they are coming from more easily.

No-one is better than, or more right than, the other.

Once you really get to know each other it's about appreciating other people for who they are and knowing you're OK. You don't have to fit into anyone else's expectations.

You can show different sides of your personality at different times and places in your life, but usually there are a couple that are more obvious, day in and day out.

Don't waste good energy trying to change the girl of your dreams or the other bloke. Learn to understand their personality.

Don't get too hung up on this – it ain't rocket science – but the understanding and acceptance of others, especially of your girl, will ensure a great and happy life together. **It's a big winner for everyone and it turns out gold.**

I said it earlier, but I want to repeat it: **Margaret and I are like chalk and cheese in our personalities – but we click. We complement each other, we accept each other, we love each other, and we don't try to change each other.**

I now know that her peaceful personality needs me to cherish and respect her feelings and show genuine love and belief in her. Otherwise I can hurt the girl I love, and that's crazy. Most of all, we love each other.

God made us all different but we're all special in our individual ways.

Understanding personalities helps us at work and at home

For the past 25 years in my business, teaching people to drive trucks, **it's been gold learning to recognise, appreciate and accept different personalities.** It's so great to help bring out the best in someone trying to learn a new skill. I can be encouraging and not get annoyed by someone's different personality.

I have learned not to rub them up the wrong way and how to enjoy my time teaching and encouraging each student. I'm sure they appreciated the change in my attitude towards them – especially when I stopped yelling!

> So, just be open to change and to new learning.
> At work,
> get on better with your colleagues and your boss.
> If you run a business,
> keep your customers
> and get the drop-outs from your competitors
> because you understand people's needs.

I reckon we should be taught about personalities in high school. It would reduce so much tension and stop anyone buckling under and/or wimping out when running into trouble with certain people. We could handle tension much better. Also **it would make meeting a girl much more pleasant!**

One of the things I've learned about the Aussie blokes I've come across is that they prefer communication one-on-one. When it comes to speaking of heart and soul issues, we're overall very shy and introverted. I must say though this can change when they're in a group or after they've been drinking alcohol.

There are numerous family stuff-ups that could have been avoided if we'd taken the time to talk and come to understand each other's personalities. Then I wouldn't have been so cut to the quick as a boy when my father and my sisters would try to shut me down with comments like, 'Be seen and not heard! Know-all, know-nothing! You're a show-off, a liar, a skite. You're up yourself.'

I'm glad I'm over all of that and can now enjoy being able to laugh at myself. I know I'm OK and I hope you know you are too.

How are you going with this one? Are you havin' a bit of a chuckle while thinking it over? Are you getting to know that you're OK? You are a champion.

Do you have a new and fresh appreciation towards the girl of your dreams, your son or daughter, where previously there may have been conflict?

God's got your picture on his fridge. You're OK.

Strengths and weaknesses

All personality types have strengths and weaknesses. No single personality type is better than any other. All have good and bad qualities, and all are needed to make this world a better place.

Whatever your temperament or personality, the Big Fella is the one who has given you the abilities and sensitivities that you possess. He has given those things to you for a purpose – that you might faithfully work at developing them and using them to do life his way.

Though our temperaments have been tainted by the cr*p of the world around us, God can show you the plan he has for you. His plan is to prosper you, not to stuff you up. It's your call though – he doesn't force anything onto you.

One of my favourite sayings is, 'The leader sets the pace of the game.'

Think about what you appreciate about personalities. You can have an interesting time thinking about all types of leaders that you liked or disliked – our political leaders, church leaders, Bible characters, school teachers you've had, your old footy coach and captain.

Now think about your footy team, your church community or your work environment. Did the personality of your leader reflect in your overall performance? Think about the leadership there, and how the members or players responded to each leader's personality.

Some players' futures live or die at the point of personality between them and their coach. Which leaders have the ability to bring out the best in all personalities and make it a winning team? **The leader sets the pace of the game.**

What's next?

Knowing what we know now about our personality from doing this little journey together, it's going to be a lot easier for us to live with and love our lovers, brothers and others – rather than wanting to hate and hurt each other. **This will stick with you for the whole of your life and will only produce gold – so enjoy.**

Make your love with the girl of your dreams amazing!

Fellas, when it is all said and done, the personality that shows out most in us represents only a small snapshot of the real-deal bloke that the Big Fella created us to be. So just enjoy your life with all the people in your life.

I know that you can expect fantastic relationships after getting the GOLD we've talked about in this chapter. **The girl of your dreams will be more special now you know how each of you tick and your real-deal dinky-di love is more beautiful.**

Champions! Make it happen.
You are the maker or breaker of your relationship.

Remember, no-one has to change your temperament or your personality. You're OK and once you appreciate the other personality types you have the GOLD. Enjoy!

TO REMEMBER

What do you look like when no-one's looking?

Learning to recognise, appreciate and accept different personalities is gold.

If someone tries to put you in a box, remember that the Big Fella's box doesn't have any lid. You can become the person he created you to be.

Character is not about loud or soft, funny or serious, it's about traits like kindness, integrity and trustworthiness.

Joy moments

HIL: *The joy of family, being the father of 3, grandfather of 8 and great grandfather of 3. Joy comes when we focus on God in our darkest or toughest moments.*

ANDREW: *Joy is just being with my wife, not doing anything special, just knowing this beautiful, talented, genuine woman is committed to doing the journey with me. When our kids show me what they've been doing, like drawing a picture. To be a helpful friend is joy. Because of the relentless pace of our lives we often miss or don't stop long enough to really enjoy our joy moments.*

MARK: *Joy is about making a change in people's lives by loving them the way God loves me.*

DUNCAN: *Joy is a bloke's life quest. It's hard to grab hold of it in large quantities. But the fleeting moments of joy are totally worth the hard work and investment.*

GAVIN: *Joy is freedom from alcohol. The wonderful reconnection with family. Not having to worry about being sober when they come over or when we go to see them. A second chance at marriage and being able to communicate and share together.*

Champion love stories

Sheila

From our first meeting there were sparks, but I thought I would marry a pastor, not a farmer. I am so thankful that Dave gave me the space I needed and didn't give up pursuing me. While our relationship hasn't been smooth sailing, I have never regretted our decision to marry.

We are both the kind of people who throw ourselves completely into whatever we are doing, and we had little 'quality' time left for each other. On top of this we had fertility issues. They were tough years.

The thing I learned about Dave and I as a team is that when difficult times arise, we are very good at supporting one another through those times.

Fast forward a few years and we had 3 children under 5 and were running 3 large farming operations. I remember thinking that it wasn't right for Dave to spend so much time away from his family. I came to resent the farming life. This attitude had a huge impact on our relationship. Finally a wise, godly woman talked to me about the unique qualities that God had placed in Dave and how he was a visionary. I was able to see that if I forced Dave into my mould, he would not be the same man. I would crush what

God had placed within him. So I gave it up and started thanking God for Dave's gifts and talents.

It is amazing how when we stop trying to control, and allow God to be God, things turn around. We both had to go through some pretty hard things, including losing everything and starting again. Dave is now home 95% of the time, and farming has become secondary to his desire to love God and serve him. I had to let go of my dreams in order to gain my heart's desire. In addition, our friendship with each other is now stronger than ever, and I am glad to say that the sparks are still there too!

Richard

When I had been married about 3 years, I was encouraged by some Christian mates to go to a men's weekend to improve our marriages. I was very sceptical but reluctantly agreed to go.

Our marriage had started off well (as they all do), but lately had seemed to bog down with a fair bit of arguing and differences of opinion, with the resultant hurt feelings and break in communication.

I would always come away from one of these exchanges muttering to myself, 'Lord, she is a beautiful woman and I love her, but why on earth is she so strong willed? She has an opinion about everything!' (No problem with me, of course).

Well, I went to this men's camp and quite liked the bloke giving the talks. A lot of practical things about how to treat your wife, *but nothing that I felt was going to make a difference to our love relationship.*

During a coffee break, I went to a table down the back of the room and cast an eye over the book titles on it. Nothing drew my interest until I came to one entitled Men & Women: Enjoying the Difference *by Dr Larry Crabb, so I bought it to take home.*

Now the interesting end to this story is that I have never read that book since I bought it 20 years ago.

But I took it home and put it on my bedside table. Over the next few weeks as my eyes beheld the title as I was coming and going, something started to gradually happen to me deep inside. I slowly became aware that I was trying to turn my wife into a clone of me. Two of 'me' living together in the same marriage – the thought shocked me to the core.

From then on, there slowly came a most beautiful transformation in our relationship. As I learned to 'forgive' my wife that her temperament and opinions were different to mine, and to release and bless her to be herself, I started to enter into the 'Enjoy' of 'Enjoying the Difference'. Now I sometimes think of her as my little Spice Rack.

AUSSIE MEN TAKE NOTE!

8. Learn patience

TO GET YOU STARTED

Through the eyes of others, how patient are you?

What is it that hampers your patience?
When and for what purpose have you shown the most patience?

Do you run on empty, or do you have your patience tank topped up ready for all occasions?

What issue in your life would improve if you were more patient?

Champions, don't take this chapter for granted. Patience is something we all need. The more we develop it, the better we will be at loving the girl of our dreams. Guaranteed!

Let's put the billy on. Pull up your comfy chair, put your feet up and have a crack at **patience** from a winner's perspective.

Without it, we'll be missing the real GOLD in all of life's challenges – especially in LOVE.

What is patience for?

The girl of your dreams can spend her whole life in fear and tension, never knowing when the next emotional explosion is about to happen. The great news, fellas, is that patience is both a learned thing, through practice, and a given – by asking God to help you. Which way for you? One, or both, it's your call.

Patience is waiting calmly for your turn.

When you're in a team and one of your blokes is a bit slow, patience is waiting for him to catch up without bawling him out.

It's showing tolerance with others. Tolerance means that you put up with something or someone, even though you may not agree with what's happening.

Tolerance means you're not always going to get your way in marriage, relationships and other areas of life.

Remember, sometimes you can think you are losing the fight but you can still win the war.

Patience and tolerance in business helps you know when to play and when to walk away. Without it, many a deal has been lost.

Bureaucratic 'bull' and some forms of political correctness test my patience. And ah, yes, what about when you're put 'on hold' and waiting to be put through to an operator about your telephone bill? **Patience**? You need plenty of it!

I face plenty of challenges every day. How about you?

What would the world around be like if we were all 10-50% more patient? I reckon it would be fantastic! Even 1% improvement would be good. **It sure would take the tension out of things.**

On the other hand we wouldn't want to be less patient by even 1%. **So we really have something here that is worth investing into.** I think we'd all want more, not less. So let me help you get the gold.

Patience is letting some things go through to the keeper. You don't have to hit every ball out of the ground. If you try, you'll end up knocking yourself out of the game. Let it go through, then shape up to the next ball.

Acting like a bulldozer all the time isn't patience, and it wears you out.

More patience in us sees the funny side of things more easily. We have a few laughs along the way and it helps bring the blood pressure down.

Sometimes it just takes me forty winks to change my attitude, and then I'm up and at 'em with fresh **patience.**

What makes you impatient?

So let's get cracking. These are a few areas that test my **patience.** It may get you thinking about what pushes your buttons.

As a truck driving instructor, I've spent many hours on the road. How do I contend with that person who cuts up on the inside ending lane pretending not to have seen the 'lane closed' sign? They then want to push in when everyone else is rolling along in turn? Ahh! That tests my **patience**!

What about the 'horn blower' behind you at the right-turn light, because you've taken 1 or 3 seconds longer to take off at the green arrow? (Impatience at the lights isn't just a bloke's problem.)

Or how about the impatient driver who tries to push you along faster, even when you're driving to the speed limit and you can't get into the left lane to get out of his road 'cause there's no space to get in?

Their impatience makes me impatient. Know what I mean? And no doubt you'll have more road incidents that get on your goat and test your **patience.**

Patience helps you hang around to listen after you've asked your woman or other family members, '**What matters most for you today**?' Their answer can give you insight into what's going on their life.

Patience in listening gives you the opportunity to get your family more connected. It can lead to the healing of any heart pains that keep couples and families apart.

> In what area of your day-to-day life
> is your patience tested?
> What sort of behaviour
> have you had trouble tolerating?
> How long can you show patience with it?

How does this play out in your family with the girl of your dreams, between fathers and sons or fathers and daughters? What other family relationships come to your mind?

Patience is powerful

In bruised, broken or battered relationships, healing can be restored or renewed with the help of patience. It may just need you to give that little bit more tolerance towards the other person, even if you don't agree with what they're saying or doing.

Sometimes you may think you've blown it, but **it's never too late to say sorry and start practising patience.**

It can help heaps to write a **'Love from your heart letter'** to the other person and restore the relationship. By just showing more **patience** you can do it. The war can still be won.

This is the story of how one champion Shed bloke wrote a 'love letter' to his son. See what you can use from it to maybe write a letter to the girl of your dreams, or someone else you love.

At a father/son Shed Night, fathers were challenged to improve the relationship they had with their sons. It was suggested that fathers could ring their sons, but it is so much better to write a letter.

- *You can write and rewrite the letter till your words are exactly right.*
- *Your son can keep the letter and read it again at any time in the future.*
- *He may treasure that letter forever.*

Disadvantages of a phone call ...

- *It may not be the best time to have that chat when you decide to ring your son.*
- *You may end the call realising you said something you wished you had not said!*
- *Your son may not remember everything you told him.*

    So I wrote a letter. Once I wrote the first draft, I gave it to Ian to read and check if it was OK to send. When he gave it back to me, he had crossed out most of what I had written saying, 'There is too much in the letter from your head, and not enough from your heart!'

I rewrote the letter and again gave it to Ian to read. This time he only crossed out half of the letter, but made a few notes asking me some 'heart' questions about what I really wanted to say to my son.

Next draft same thing, but much less crossed out. **My son received version 12!** It included an apology for anything I had done through his childhood that was a bit harsh or unjust with regard to discipline. I asked for his forgiveness. I told him that I loved him very much and how proud I am of him.

Ian said to send the letter without expecting any response. I thought he was right, because more than a week went by with no response.

However, early the next week my son rang to say that he had been away and was delighted to receive my letter! He sounded a bit emotional as he went through the various parts of the letter.

You may have been waiting patiently for the girl of your dreams or that son or daughter to change for the better, and nothing much is happening. You may need to give a little more ground. That's tolerance.

The breakthrough could be closer than you think. Always consider giving up the right to get even.

But you've gotta wanna!

Learning patience for Watto and Margaret

Once you come to understand how you and others tick, you will see the need for patience in all relationships.

Margaret and I have had to learn this. She has always been a patient person, but early in our marriage even her patience was stretched by my involvement in the footy!

Margaret says...

Keeping meals warm 3 nights a week (no microwaves back then), the weekly matches and the drawn-out presentations after the game were things I had to get used to as part of our life together. Later, Ian started a new club in the suburbs, which meant coaching, pie nights, meetings, fundraising and social get-togethers.

Our eldest son started playing at 5. When our 3 sons played, Saturday mornings were taken up driving all over Brisbane. I didn't mind this so much as I saw how good it was for the boys. But as well as this, Ian became involved in the Queensland under-17s as team manager, coach and selector. This took him away for several weeks, interstate, each year.

It's not that I dislike sports – I played tennis for many years and took up golf at age 50. But I do need to exercise patience when football takes over and there's no time for much else – especially jobs around the house!

I had to learn to be considerate. I've had to learn to be patient with Margaret, too – like when she's not ready to get up in the morning!

I think 6.30 is a reasonable time to get up unlike *someone* who likes to get up at 4.30 or earlier!

So I try to get up quietly now, and I don't take her breakfast in bed – she'd probably throw it at me! Haha.

With the right attitude you can have fun and enjoy putting patience into practice. We've had plenty of good laughs with each other along the way.

If I'm in a hurry, sometimes I say to Margaret, 'Love, just do it your way.' Margaret can get cut by my sharp reply, and think I'm having a dummy spit. I don't want a discussion, but she wants a conversation with plenty of listening by me and discussion. My impatience can be taken the wrong way and she can be put off. So I must think before I speak to her.

I often say to Ian that a conversation isn't a competition where there's a winner – where either of us does it "my way". We still need lots of practice with this one and it all takes time, lots of it. Pretty hard for a man who's always on the move but we'll keep at it and hopefully improve!

There was one really big issue where we both had to learn patience. I'll let Margaret tell the story.

Margaret says...

Margaret says, 'I went to church every Sunday, but Ian wasn't interested in coming with me, and I didn't like going alone. Once our first son was born I wanted to bring him up to know Jesus so I started going to a monthly women's group. Some older Christian women nurtured me and other young mothers.

I began growing closer to Jesus. I joined another group of women who met weekly for Bible study. I now wanted Ian to get to know Jesus better and so started pestering him to come to church with me. Of course, that didn't work.

I reminded God that he had said Ian was for me when I wanted a Christian husband. So I started praying for him.

By this time, all our boys were in primary school. I had been taking them to Sunday School but they were becoming more resistant each week. They wanted to stay home with Dad who was having much more fun on a Sunday morning with friends who came to see his horses.

My patience was running very thin.

I'd heard about a friend who was learning more about the Holy Spirit and whose life had changed. I was curious. I prayed fervently for the Holy Spirit to make any changes necessary in me.

One night, while everyone was fast asleep, I had the experience of a bright light coming into the room. It was overwhelming. I didn't know what it was all about, and I certainly didn't know what was to come from that night.

Ian had been really unhappy about my involvement in Bible study groups. He had felt he was losing me to God. In desperation, he too cried out to God to reveal himself – he needed to know if God was real for himself.

God answered us both. He showed his power at work by the change his Spirit made in me. Although Ian knew I'd always loved him, there was a new love coming out of me from my changed heart, one that had been touched by the Spirit of God. And that power through me touched Ian also.

Our walk following Jesus together has had many challenges. We've learned to grow together in the different expressions of our spirituality. We've had to learn to discuss many issues to eventually come to a place where we accept each other, so our unique gifts can develop and flow together and out to others.'

Wow! Pow! We got the gold – but it took patience. Don't give up!

Champions, we all need to learn patience!

You can blow the girl of your dreams, your son or daughter-in-law out of the ballpark 'cause they haven't grown up doing life your way. Remember, if you go at things like a bulldozer, that hurts heaps.

Patience is needed. Respect their upbringing and their point of view. You may need patience and the gentleness of a feather to get the best of the situation and win their confidence.

Patience: It's waiting, there for the taking.

Champion, if you're having a bit of a battle with impatience sometimes it's best to take yourself out of the rat race. Just 'smell the roses', drop in a fishing line, have a day watching a bit of cricket or tennis on the telly, or just be still for a moment.

Allow those little niggly frustrations to go through to the keeper.

This can help you **get rid of stinkin' thinkin'** and **give up the need to get even. Time out can help you learn patience.**

Champion, how long is your fuse? What pushes your buttons? Sometimes it doesn't take much to blow our fuse and send us into intolerance and impatience. It usually depends on what mood we're in at the moment.

> Don't get me wrong –
>   I'm not saying you just roll over and give in.
> There are things you need to hold fast against,
> and be able to walk away from – or run – if necessary.
>
> Slow and steady wins the race. Patience!

Patience in business

In my early days as a truck driver trainer when I was still learning heaps, I had a bloke who was really hard work. I didn't look forward to his next lesson, but he taught me one of my greatest lessons in **patience**.

After obtaining his licence he took off to work in the mines. Down the track I began getting this high flow of students from one particular mining company, only to discover that it all started with the bloke who tested my patience.

He recommended me to his mining company, to be their preferred provider – get it? True story! All it took was for me to learn **patience** to give my students my best. Then he taught me. How's that for gold?

Sometimes the customer, colleague or boss you wouldn't have chosen can turn out to be a blessing in disguise. This bloke became my teacher!

Small business has been very challenging over the past few years. Companies are finding things tighter and tougher. Customers become more important. Much more **patience** is needed to ensure they do continuing business with your company.

You can be forced into being more tolerant of them, and using prices and after-sales service to win your share of a tougher market. If it doesn't kill you, eventually it can be better for you.

You can do much better business and make more money. But if you are pig-headed and impatient you will lose them.

Mate, just pause and have a red-hot think before you shoot your mouth off.

Once you learn to be more **patient** with people in one particular area of your life it can quickly flow into other areas. You'll notice that any pride, anger or selfishness you may have had will drop off. You'll develop the ability to face the battles of the day better. **You can turn general inquiries into sales and you'll keep the blood pressure down.**

Patience at home

How short is your fuse? What pushes your buttons when it comes to the girl of your dreams?

How are you at the end of a big day
where you needed heaps of patience with others
and then come home to the ones you love the most?

Do you drop
the level of tolerance and patience towards them,
 or kick it up a notch?
It needs to be the latter.
 They should get the preferential treatment.
 They do the hard yards of life with you.

You can do it! Best of all, be consistent – you'll feel better in the long run. Acting like a pork chop doesn't do anyone any good. If Margaret's had a hard and challenging day, she appreciates me coming home with **patience**.

You can do it!

The times I showed a hothead attitude as a young husband or father didn't help Margaret or our 3 sons. It just shut them down.

I told you before that I didn't always show patience in my boys' horseriding or surfing, but one area that I did learn to show patience was footy. When I learned to kick the ball myself, I learned it wrong, and I could never get rid of the bad habit. So I patiently taught each son to get it right with their kicking or handballing, and they still kick the ball well as men.

It brought joy to my heart when one of them told me recently that I have always been patient with their Big Statements, Big Opinions, and Big Business Ideas. He reckons I never hold them back to this day from speaking out their dreams and opinions on all subjects. They have strong opinions and we don't always agree, but I have tried never to call them anything less than champions.

Patience from a young husband and father brings life and sparkle into your family. Patience with each child, letting them move at their own pace, helps the creativity come out. It allows their personality to show through.

Don't make the ones you love miss out.

**Patience is powerful!
Don't make the ones you love miss out on it.**

This is Men's stuff not Boy's stuff. Champions, let's step up to the plate and make real-deal love happen.

How to become more patient

I was a bit of a hothead as a young bloke. I grew up with a bad temper and wanted my way instantly. I didn't have a clue about **patience**.

Thankfully, my dad had his 'attitude adjuster' and he gently and tactfully knocked me into reality. Ha ha!

He turned my bad-sport attitude around to help me become a determined young achiever. Dad helped me grow a lot of stickability. He patiently and consistently helped me develop.

Where else can a bloke get a bit of help?

There's a beauty in the *Work Manual* that goes like this:

> Unless the Big Fella builds the house,
> You blokes who build the house do it in vain;
> Unless the Big Fella keeps his eye on the job,
> The blokes you have looking after it may as well stay in bed asleep. (Psalm 127:1, Watto Version)

The older I become the more convinced I am that we bash ourselves trying to do it in our own strength. We have a choice to get the Top Man to be the project manager all the way.

I did everything in my own strength until my head ached. It took lots of **patience** for me to learn to trust God.

Let's look for a moment at the big picture. How do you think we are going as a country? I reckon we're doing it mighty tough, and we don't need to.

After many years of lookin', listenin' and learnin' I have a saying that goes like this: **'Deny the spiritual part of who you are at your own peril.'** This becomes gold when you can address it – in any area of your life.

How about another bit of gold **from the *Work Manual*:**

**But the fruit of God's Spirit is
love, joy, peace, PATIENCE,
kindness, goodness, faithfulness,
gentleness, self-control.**
(Galatians 5:22 Watto Version)

These are gifts from God's Spirit to our spirits. But because he gave us a free will, we need to open our hearts and spirits. We need to be recharged with **patience to** keep open and keep flowing.

You just need to take it aboard into your spirit. It's your call. Nobody else can do it for you.

I'm glad I am constantly challenged in the spiritual part of me. I still face little battles and have many things to learn, but I'm much happier and more contented.

Getting to the spiritual part of life

No-one pushes you into the spiritual area of who you are. No-one pushed me. You have to go there yourself.

Champions, I want to highlight this point. 'A man convinced against his will remains the same man still' says the author Dale Carnegie – a wise saying!

So I'm not going to push you into it. **But I also don't want you pushed *away*. I want you to have all the facts so that you can make your own call when you choose.**

You might look around and think Aussie blokes aren't very spiritual. But I've discovered we prefer to talk one-on-one about these issues. We're spiritual, but very shy to talk openly about spiritual things.

In today's world, we choose to go big on the mind and the body. There are gyms everywhere, plenty of personal trainers, and much more available to help us get a healthy and fit body.

And how much do we spend these days on the latest superfood? Think about how many new diets, cookery books and TV shows are available.

And for the mind? We're paying big bucks in education and private coaching for our problems, and there are plenty of therapists and life coaches to help us. All this is great and we also have shelves of books or websites telling us how to be successful and make a million. **We live in the land of plenty – yet the use of anti-depressants and the need for mental health care is on the increase. This is a huge worry.**

What's missing?

What we need desperately is more help in this third area – the spiritual part of life.

We've lost it here big time! Unfortunately so many have been derailed by thinking that spirituality is a lot of religious rules and sitting in a church on Sunday.

I used to think like that. I missed out on the relationship part of the Father and the Son bit – God the Father, Jesus the Son.

In fact, it's about meeting the Top Man – God – on a first-name basis, getting to know his Son, Jesus, and doing life together. He also gives us his Spirit to work changes in us on the inside.

Have a good think about this one. Be patient – you could be in for a pleasant surprise.

Don't be afraid to HAVE A CRACK at the spiritual part of you.

I've watched and listened to thousands of men all trying hard to be human, and being so very, very shy in their spirit.

But I've come to know that
when men are safe
and know they are not going to be knocked
   or judged,
   they are very spiritual.
They can talk about heart and soul issues
   very comfortably.   That's gold!

It's not about being religious!

When people ask me what religion I am, I say, 'I follow **Carlton (AFL).'** Talking footy, our last 2 seasons have tested my **patience**! But I'm loyal, so I'm prepared to tolerate our new game plan for this season. I hope it pays off. That's my religion!

Stop press: I now also follow North Melbourne, since my grandson, Declan Watson, was drafted – No. 35!

And when they say, 'No, I mean what church do you go to?' I say, 'I'm not telling you 'cause then we'll talk all day in churchy lingo about denominational differences and other church stuff.'

So I say, 'You mean Jesus, the Bloke?' and when they say, 'Yes' – well, that conversation is one worth having.

> He's made me keep it simple
> and go straight to Him
> and not get lost along the way – no middleman.
> I talk to the Big Fella, tell him all my stuff,
> the good and bad,
> the happy or sad.

I can talk out loud (if I'm by myself), or silently inside my head, and he hears me either way. I can be anywhere – at home, the car, at work. It doesn't have to be a special place. Try it! And make sure you keep your eyes open if you're driving your car or truck or riding ya horse!

I ask him what his plan is for what I'm going to do, and how he thinks I should tackle it. Again, **God's ways and thoughts are bigger and better than Watto's ways and thoughts** (**Isaiah 55:8–9**).

I also ask him for help to sort out any of my stuff-ups, and so I can take aboard more **patience** and tolerance.

I'll keep doing this until he takes me home when he's finished with me here on earth.

So mate, if and when you want to see whether you are a spiritual being trying to be human, just call out to him and ask the Big Fella if he's for real.

Keep your radar up and just keep asking him to show you in your life, not anybody else's. Enjoy the challenge! It's your call. Have **patience**!

What about you, champion?

This is a well-known saying:

> Patience is a virtue,
> Get it if you can,
> Seldom in a woman,
> Never in a man.

After 50 years with Margaret, I think **'seldom'** in a woman should be **'mostly'** in a woman – that's how they appear to me. **How patient do women have to be, going through 9 months of pregnancy and giving birth?** Wow, I'm glad I'm a bloke.

What if we blokes have a crack at this one, and kick it up by 50%?

What if we open our minds and hearts to accept the Big Fella's full dose of his **patience**? What if we could change the 'never in a man' to **'always in a man'**? How good would the world around us be!

So come on, show patience! Have a crack! Think about it. What could you do differently?

> **A Watto tip:** It's vital to spend special one-on-one quality time with the girl of your dreams. It doesn't necessarily mean a date, but it could be just sitting together over a meal or coffee, watching the moon, or going on a road trip. It's about getting away from your usual life just to be with the one you love or are trying to love. Put the phone down and saturate each other in quality time and quantity time, and you're guaranteed to become better mates and dinky-di lovers.

About horses and patience...

As I've mentioned, one of my favourite movies is *The Horse Whisperer,* starring Robert Redford. It's a story about a horse that has been hit by a truck and ends up very badly wounded and spooked.

Then when the horse meets the horse whisperer it comes back to reality without the use of any bashing, bullying or cruelty. The horse whisperer helps the traumatised horse back to life with love, gentleness, much tolerance and **patience**.

He just hangs in with the crazed horse until it reaches that moment of trust.

The horse first sees the horse whisperer as his predator. But then in time the connection, **trust and patience begin to** happen with much love from within – and that wins the day.

The gold is got when the horse reaches the moment of trust to be helped out of fear and trauma.

The horse whisperer applies the same patience to the girl who was riding the horse when the accident happened, as well as her mother. The gold is got there also.

It's **a fantastic movie about tolerance and patience.** It helps me heaps as I apply the horse whisperer principle to my relationships.

I've repeated this story so that you'll have a really good think about it. Could you learn from it too?

But you've just gotta wanna! You can learn it!

Are you more like the horse, or more like the horse whisperer? Maybe it's a bit of both. Many of us can be wounded or spooked by things in the past.

Have a fair dinkum look at yourself. Be **patient** in letting people come to you instead of pushing them away.

They'll learn to trust you, and you'll learn to trust them. They'll also be attracted towards you. Mighty good results will show all around you, and you'll get the gold!

> There's always more to a story.
> Don't push.
> Let people come to you!

So don't run away in selfishness or spit it. Learn more **patience**. See the stars, not the bars, in the larger picture of life. Keep close to people who display much **patience** – it can be caught and taught.

You're never too old to learn **by watching both those with it and those without it. Learn from the bad and take in the good!**

Don't end up a miserable, lonely, grumpy old bloke. Come on, you can do it! You end up with the gold! The girl of your dreams will love you more, the more **patient you become**.

When we can't see our children

Another area where blokes struggle big time is when they can't see their children following a **break-up**. A bloke's mind is in complete chaos. **Patience** soon flies out the window.

Where do you go for help and guidance? To the family, to another person who has been there before, to the family law solicitor?

You might spend plenty of money and have paperwork to prove your entitlement and you still can't see your children. What next?

How's your **patience** now you are in uncharted waters? Do you have any left? How long will it be before you explode?

Too many good people get smashed in this area because of frustration, ignorance, *impatience and intolerance*. And that can only spell disaster.

So fellas, first port of call …

Put the billy on and sit back and think, 'My way out or the spiritual way out?' Ask for more **patience** from the One who can help you here. There is so much hurt and pain on both sides that also needs to be considered.

Because of the differences in personality and temperament, each person in the break-up will process things in his or her own particular way.

Forgiveness is vital to healing and emotional health but some may take a long time – even years – to consider forgiving the other person, because of betrayal.

Give that family member a lot of space. Exercise more **patience**, and the outcome will be much healthier all round.

> There are always three sides to every story.
> 1. Mine
> 2. Yours
> 3. The Bloke Upstairs listening to both of us
>   – the truth.

Fellas, if you experienced separation in your marriage when your children were very young, as they grow up and go through different stages you may need much **patience** to allow them the space to do so.

You can lose them by trying to keep them as your little-girl princess or your little-boy champion that they were at the time of the break-up. Allow them to go through the stages of growing up. It may be painful at times when they choose not to spend time with you.

Keep on loving them. Try to maintain respect for their mother. Through your patient attitude you'll keep the door open for a continuing relationship with them into adulthood.

An encouraging word to turbocharge your patience!

Let's finish this chapter off with a bit more gold from the *Work Manual*:

> **My brothers, count it a joy when you fall into various trials knowing that testing of your faith produces patience. But let patience have its perfect work that you may be perfect and complete, lacking nothing. (James 1:2–4)**

Champions! You can do all the courses on love, but if you haven't got patience you're only doing pretend love.

So enjoy the challenge and have courage in learning to have great patience and love more!

TO REMEMBER

Patience is powerful – it can heal a battered relationship, and turn good love into great love.

It's never too late to learn patience.

Try writing a 'love letter' from the heart to your loved one.

Joy moments

OTTO: *Being confident that all will turn out well and we get to kick that winning goal after the siren.*

CHRIS: *An inner knowing that I have been restored to right relationship with my Heavenly Dad, through Jesus. Gives me strength to be the husband and father God wants me to be, to be a mate. Helps me to be a human being, not a human doing.*

WAYNE: *I count it all joy looking after my son who is quadriplegic.*

MATT: *Patience leads to joy.*

STEVE: *Joy is living out God's desires for me as opposed to the world's desires or the desires of others forced upon me.*

DAVO: *Joy for me is connection with friends/mates. It means having friends who stand by you and who you stand by. Our first response to tough times is, 'God, rescue me!' but God wants to show us instead that he is bigger than our adversity. God wants to walk with you today however tough the journey is.*

Champion love stories

Grace

We were that couple who were crazy, passionately, head-over-heels in love. With the birth of our first child, all of a sudden I didn't really know who I was. My name, hormones, body, job and lifestyle had all changed dramatically.

Our relationship wasn't exciting dates and holidays anymore but sleep deprivation and boring chores. It was a period of grinding gears, quarrels, confusion and conflict.

I went from being independent, capable and accomplished in my professional life, to being at home all day with a baby, doing jobs that quickly came undone. When Toby would leave for work in the morning I felt jealous that he got to go out and 'have a life'.

During those first few years, I often got frustrated with Toby. It brought out a bitter, critical side of me. He would go quiet. I questioned whether I had married the right guy.

After the birth of our second baby, I was diagnosed with postnatal anxiety. In the course of getting professional help, we did a stocktake on our life. We realized that we were doing too much, spending our precious resources of time and energy on things which weren't nurturing our marriage or family.

Toby had to accept that he didn't know how to fix the problem. None of the tools he had could change the situation, and he realized that he needed to learn to care for me. This involved a lot of listening and empathising.

I was completely vulnerable and weak and I had to learn to accept help from Toby, to lean on him and trust him.

We prayed, we made changes and slowly we started to rebuild our life. Ultimately, it was our mutual vulnerability which led to the transformation of our marriage. For our marriage to thrive, we needed to put it first, and to maintain it as a safe place, no matter how we were doing.

I realized that whether I valued my husband was not dependent on what he had done but on my attitude towards him. I realised I was the maker or breaker of my own marriage.

I began to try and set Toby up to win. In encouraging him and praising him for his God-given abilities and traits, I watched him flourish. He was able to do more and be more and of course was more affectionate. This made me want to keep cherishing him and in turn he would respond positively.

7 years later, we have 4 children, some chooks and a whole different relationship. We are more connected, more in love and feel more blessed than ever before. We continue to be curious about understanding one another and picking up new tools in our relationship. Toby is a solid leader in our marriage whilst still respecting and encouraging my strengths.

We are imperfect people, forever flawed. But we believe anyone can choose to transform their relationship by laying down their habit of self-protection and adopting a practice of vulnerability. This requires asking God to come into every part of your relationship, but the result is always love and unity.

9. Encourage each other

> **TO GET YOU STARTED**
>
> If you don't know how to encourage your girl and she doesn't know how to encourage you, you'll end up like a dried-up prune.
>
> If you can give encouragement, it will come back to you, and you're going to get even more heaped on you. Wow! It's gold!

Champions, for me this is the most enjoyable part of my book. In doing the journey of love with the girl of your dreams, **encouragement is an absolute must.**

Margaret and I have worked at encouraging each other to a wonderful place of trust. The Big Fella has shaped us over 50 years into love and encouragement.

We both know that we say what we mean and we mean what we say, and therefore we have joy together. I hope you will enjoy a similar journey in love. Be encouraged. It's worth it.

Does it come naturally?

I'm a natural-born encourager and because it's easy for me to give it, it's easy for me to teach you how receive it and pass it on to others.

> **Seriously, can anyone get by without encouragement? I don't believe they can.**
>
> **I reckon most people have to survive**
>   **on the smallest amount.**
> **This need not be the case**
>   **– it can be changed.**

So, how do you get more encouragement? Once you learn to give encouragement, eventually it will come back to you in bucket loads.

If you haven't grown up in a house full of encouragement then this can be new to you. That's OK, we'll sort it out so that you can enjoy this most exciting gift. It doesn't take much!

Who would have thought that my saying, **'I've never seen a bloke go backwards with encouragement'** would have helped so many blokes to become real-deal champions?

I now hear it said in all corners of our country, and people love hearing and saying it. I hope you like it and want to spread it. Yes, that's how my first book *Every Bloke's a Champion – Even You!* began.

In that book, I got to suss out some gold I had picked up along my journey through life and share it. When a man is treated like a champion, he starts living like one. And so does a woman!

No-one misses out on the battle

I say life's a battle and no-one misses out. It's just got a different name and time. It's how you handle the battle that counts.

Our day-to-day living can be a much harder battle without that little bit of encouragement. It can be mighty tough if we're going to constantly cop judgement, criticism or the silent 'no-speakie' treatment. It's pretty tough to keep getting back up from that, especially from the one we are trying to love. Does your woman do that to you?

But then, do you do it to her?

My business life was set alight by my treasured mate, big Jonesy, empowering me when he said, 'Watto you'll never look back!' And I haven't. How's that for encouragement?

Have you ever experienced a word like that? Perhaps you have but you may have missed it? Let's help you to be ready for the next turbocharged word of encouragement coming your way.

Once you know how healthy it is to receive an encouraging word and how it puts a turbocharge into your whole being, you'll want to learn how to give encouragement to others so you can see them charge off onwards and upwards. It's so exciting and the gold starts to happen.

It doesn't take much, just a little word from someone we respect. **Right at this moment, who is it that's in your thoughts or on your mind? Why not pick up the phone** and say, 'Howdy. I've been thinking about you. How's it going?' Then listen carefully and give a kind word of encouragement. I guarantee you'll make that person's day. A text message also works well – and for the girl of your dreams it's worth double gold!

From the *Work Manual*… how good!

> Nothing is more appealing
> than speaking beautiful, life-giving words,
> for they release sweetness to our souls,
> inner healing to our spirits.
> (Proverbs 16:24 TPT)

We all want and need encouragement. It can make us, or the lack of it can break us.

Encouragement is sorta like a plant in the garden. Keep the water and the right sunshine up to it and it keeps looking better and better.

No water, no encouragement – the plant withers up and dies. It's a plant but it's dead. We can be like that. We can get around, but we're a dead man walkin'.

> **Encouragement comes in so many different ways**
>   **and it's the most amazing thing.**
> **It's pretty normal for us blokes to need**
> **an affirming, encouraging word from another man, no matter how old we are.**
> **If you try this, remember,**
>   **blokes like you to call it as it is**
>   **– straight down the line,**
>   **with no patronising.**

When you're fishing, what keeps you there? Usually, a nibble! That gives you encouragement to keep casting out and keeping your bait fresh.

No bite? How long before you move on?

What are some of the things that encourage you? I reckon we could quickly and easily fill a page if we stop and think of the people and things around us.

Because encouragement works for both blokes and women, let's ramp up this saying: **'I've never seen anyone go backwards with encouragement'.** As a matter of fact, when you get or give dinky-di encouragement, you will know for sure that **you'll never see anyone die from over-praise, over-love or over-encouragement.**

We can change the world with encouragement.

It's all about communication

A great deal of successful real-deal love comes from good communication. In fact, it is the key.

This is worth repeating: **A great deal of successful real-deal love comes from good communication. In fact, it is the key.**

Ensure the girl of your dreams feels safe to put her ideas into the mix. You will learn not to force her into silence or anger by the way you raise a point, and instead have a good and fair chat.

Learn how to tell your story and how to invite your loved one to tell her story. Keep on track and don't lose it! Get the best results for both of you.

A Watto Tip:

- Watch the tone of your voice. It can be cruel or kind.
- Think before you speak.
- Think and speak from your heart.

This little beauty works – when your woman tells you something important ask her to repeat it.

I'm going to repeat this: When your woman tells you something important ask her to repeat it. Margaret loves me doing this 'cause she knows she has my full attention.

Usually we blokes listen the first time in our head and have a quick answer or want to rush off to instantly fix the problem.

When we get the girl of our dreams to repeat it, we can listen in our heart. After that we can get our head and heart together. Out comes the gold, and we keep coming up with great solutions together.

Once I got this going with Margaret she came closer to me. She knew that I cared about her thoughts – that's encouragement.

Encouragement makes our hearts go 'ping!'

Everyone needs turbocharged affirming words. We all long to know we're especially loved and cherished. How are you at speaking these encouraging words for your girl? Here's some ideas!

- If your girl has had a trip to the hairdresser, a nice word of admiration helps make nice heart-love.
- 'Wow! That perfume sure smells moreish.'
- 'You look great! That style really suits you', or 'You look so good in that colour.' In case you want to buy her some clothing, know what colours suit her and know her size so you don't bring home something too small!
- Every so often chocolates are like gold. But make sure you know the right brand and whether it's milk or dark that's preferred.
- Know whether she drinks tea or coffee and how she has it. Or whether it's to be a hot or cold chocolate.
- Empower your woman with praise and she'll fly you to the moon. Know what I mean?
- **Tell her how much you love her, OFTEN.**
- **Appreciate her for what she stands for and what she means to you, or how she has helped you to be the real-deal man.**
- **Remember to keep the girl of your dreams' updated picture on the screen of your phone.**

Get your priorities in order – wife, children, job, then other stuff. Get this out of whack and you pay a price.

If you acknowledge the spiritual part of you, you will put the Big Fella first and include him in everything. This was a big step for me to take, but God gently showed me how to get the gold in love after I put him first – then Margaret.

Take a serious look at this. If you don't get this order right, the wheels can fall off. **Let's face it, this is one of the hardest things to get right.** I wish I'd learned it sooner.

Fellas, watch out for hurtful words

We blokes can sometimes say things that we think are funny or smart but are really hurtful to women. I'll list some as a warning for 'danger ahead'.

Margaret says...

For any girls, young or old like me, all this applies for us too regarding our men. Just make the appropriate word changes as you read.

- **If you criticise or talk her down you won't even get real-deal love off the ground.** Be careful if you start making judgements or negative comments about her, or about people or things that are important to her. If you're not aware of your woman's particular struggles or special needs, you can be criticising her and making her feel very hurt and wondering why.

- It's possible to make her feel shame, especially if you are finding fault with her looks, her body parts or her shape. But if she's been dieting, make sure you encourage and compliment her.

- Don't criticise or try some smart remark in public at the expense of the girl of your dreams and hope she picks up a hint about something. If you have something to say, do so in private – gently. Give praise in public.

- **Don't complain about and criticise your in-laws. Your wife can't change them.**

- **Don't rubbish her close girlfriends. They don't have to be your friends, nor do their husbands need to be your friends. Sometimes this is just the way it is. Realise that women need women friends for women talk.**

- **Don't knock her spirituality if you're not there yet. That will hurt her heaps and affects her intimacy with you. She will feel hurt in her heart.**

- **Same goes for you, mate, if you're the spiritual one – no preaching at her, no unreal expectations or pushing her into your way of thinking. She must learn in her own way and time. Loving her through your individual journeys and together-journey is your only call.**

- **Champions, have a serious look at this! Don't commit spiritual adultery on the girl of your dreams. What I mean by this is that I don't tell another woman deep and meaningful stuff that I must talk over with Margaret first. Then, only if she agrees, it is OK to share with other women.** If you share deep, heart issues with another woman such as your secretary or someone who works closely with you, you begin to connect in your heart with that person. That hurts your relationship with your wife and hinders her love for you. A heart connection can lead to more. It took me a while to realise that Margaret didn't appreciate me sharing my feelings with other women before telling her.

- Another area that needs to be looked at in marriage is when a bloke thinks he's being smart by making reference to his wife by his mother-in-law's Christian name, because he thinks she's acting like her mother and he doesn't like it. **Don't take cheap shots at the girl of your dreams at the expense of your mother-in-law.** Blokes, you may think it's funny but most times our women hate it. It can make them cranky. She may be struggling to break free of those things in her mother that she doesn't want. Be sensitive. There's a spiritual consequence and blessing, too. **The *Work Manual* says 'all' goes well if you honour your ma and pa!** (Exodus 20:12, Deuteronomy 5:16)

- Cut out the religiosity and church stuff full of rules and have-to's. Don't be Mr Perfect in church circles and someone else in the home. Be consistent in your behaviour. It's in the home where it counts.

- No trying to pick up someone at the sleazy lust part of town, or having it off with your mate's wife behind his back. No sexting to a third party. All these types of things and more have huge consequences. You will miss real-deal dinky-di love.

Encouragement can take different forms

One of my mates recently lost his only daughter in a car smash. Can you imagine how wrecked he and his wife felt? I shook his hand, gave him a gentle blokey hand on the shoulder, and encouraged him to talk out his pain and grief as he needed. He said that some days, he just can't move.

We became mates way back, through our interest in racehorses and trying to pick winners from time to time. I don't bother with going to the TAB now, but he does. I told him his daughter would be smiling in heaven if she knew he occasionally took a treble, and to keep doing stuff that made him feel good.

Gentle encouragement from my heart was what I gave him. He didn't need a big lecture, or some big story about my woes. All that was needed was an encouraging word.

A Watto tip: A hug or a hand on the shoulder can be a great encourager. At one father-and-son Shed Night I said, 'If you haven't given your son a manhug and told them you love them in the past week, do it now.' They all sat there and looked at me, and I told them to get over it. A lot of blokes there would have loved that encouraging touch. It's healthy, and we often don't get enough of it. And don't forget, touch is especially important in your relationship with the girl of your dreams. We all prefer to give or get love in different ways. A woman or man who is 'huggy' and never gets touched is starved. I'm huggy and Margaret isn't – but this part of our relationship is strong because we know what each other needs. Don't be selfish or ignorant in this area with the girl of your dreams. Just make it happen!

How are you going with this little gem? In the *Work Manual* it says, '**Don't hold back encouragement when it's within your power to do it**' **(Proverbs 3:27, Watto Version).**

One of my young mates from Shed sent me a little note of encouragement the other day.

He wrote, 'Hey Watto, a mate was telling me how well his store is going. He's been promoted to Store Manager. He said the reason his staff are going so well is because of this message I'd sent him about encouragement.' He had applied it to his store and started passing it onto his staff team. **Because of the encouraging atmosphere in this small store they're getting better sales than ever before.**

The workers 'got it'. They knew the encouragement was the real deal. They took it aboard and got the gold.

On the other hand, there's always someone ready to pounce on you with a mouthful if you make a mistake.

It doesn't take much to learn discouragement. Just look at the evening news on television and you can be dragged down by all that negativity before your eyes. Sadly, our politicians seem to think it's their sole purpose to discourage each other constantly.

My solution is to turn off your telly, or only watch shows that build you, not destroy you.

What about you, champion?

So let's speak out the gold from our hearts and let the encouragement flow. No 'fluffy duck' patronising stuff, just give out plain old-fashioned encouragement – it's the gold! Come on mate, you can do it.

Start with a little word. You don't have to yell it out. Just eyeball the person if you can and encourage them. Be real.

There are countless opportunities right there in front of you all the time. You can do it! **Say what you mean and mean what you say.** Especially to the girl of your dreams – she'll blossom with love and encouragement!

Champions, if you live like an island, all alone, and you keep looking inwards, you have no-one to give encouragement to, and there's no-one around to encourage you. We're not built like that. That's not what life's all about.

Come on, you can do it! But you've gotta wanna.

Even one liners work well to encourage. Try some of these, especially with the girl of your dreams:

> Well done!   Great stuff!   Thanks a lot!
> Thanks!   I'm pumped!
> Come on, you can do it!   You were great!
> You do that well!   Have a crack!
> You're a champion!   I want to be in your team!
> You make that outfit look great!
> That's gold!   You're a winner!   Super-duper!
> Luv ya, mate!   Hi, Princess!
> Mate, I'll pay to fill your car at the bowser.

Those times when you receive encouraging, complimentary words, just say thank you. Believe it, accept it, and get on with it.

Boy! It doesn't take much encouragement from Margaret to light my fire.

Learning how to receive encouragement

Who and what lights your fire with encouragement?

Fellas, it takes a little courage to get this gold flowing, but remember 'little fish are sweet'. No pain, no gain – inch by inch is a cinch, yard by yard is too hard.

I've received words of encouragement from people all around the country after someone has given them a copy of *Every Bloke's a Champion – Even You!* They've told me how it has helped them sort out some of life's past cr*p that has been holding them back from becoming the real-deal champion. It has encouraged them on their journey in life, making a significant difference for the better.

How encouraging to receive an email, a hand-written card, a letter in the post with a stamp on it, a phone call or text, or when I'm at a Shed night somewhere around the country and a bloke comes up and thanks me for writing my books.

Encouragement from both men and women is great to receive. Encouragement works wonders for me and I'm sure it does for you too.

Sadly many people are starved of encouragement – and too often it's the girl of your dreams. When you say something encouraging or pay them a compliment they don't know how to accept it. They may reply that you're a charmer or wonder if you want something from them.

This attitude can discourage you from giving them further encouragement. Obviously they're not used to someone saying something nice to them, especially in a love relationship.

On a flight recently, I heard a flight attendant say some lovely, encouraging and polite words to a passenger seated in front of me. When that flight attendant came to me I told her it was really nice to hear how politely she encouraged the other passenger. I said, 'Well done!'

The flight attendant couldn't handle it at first and suspected that I was trying to get favour from her. After realising that I meant what I said, she lit up like a fancy dress ball. She knew that I wasn't after anything or trying to win her heart.

If you encourage you'll often find you'll receive favour because people respond to genuine encouragement. They're grateful to receive it and want to be around you. The girl of your dreams will light up like she's swallowed the sun.

> A straightforward word from your heart
> to someone you care about
>   goes straight into their heart.
> They'll know that they're loved and cared for by you.
> They can then bite the bullet
>   and move forward.

Champions, keep coming on this little journey through my book and get the gold. I write this from a practical hands-on part of life that has worked for me where the rubber hits the road. This is no information download theory read. I wish this book to be a 'make it happen' winner. Giving encouragement is now a natural part of every conversation for Margaret and me.

Can a hard word be encouraging?

You may think a hard word can be encouraging, but if the person you're speaking to doesn't feel loved and respected by you, your word will be damaging and discouraging. They'll feel they're just being pounded and discouraged.

When I was 20, I was cruising in a happy place with love from Margaret, and my footy going great. Then my birthdate came out of the draw for 2 years' conscription for military service. When I went through the 12 weeks of basic training it was a major shock, to say the least. I didn't want to be there.

Encouragement! No way! I was constantly yelled at, abused, bullied and belittled. Treated like a number, not a person, and stripped of my identity. I felt like a sausage just punched out of the sausage factory. I felt like I'd done something really bad and they were getting square.

Maybe if the armed forces had let us know at the start that it was designed to sort people out for the pressure of the frontline battle, their basic training would have been more acceptable.

But I finished it with a king-size chip on my shoulder, and set about doing the bare minimum. **For lots of years afterwards I carried judgement about anyone misusing a position of authority.**

Compare it to my footy experience: I played from under-12s until I was 24 years old. In that time I had many coaches with different personalities. Because we were trying to win a game of footy we always received encouragement from the coach, not abuse.

Even the coach's occasional three-quarter-time blast was given in a manner to bring out the best and not to discourage. What a shame my military instructors didn't learn how to do that!

Mate, if my story hits a chord, take a moment to consider your own place of discouragement.

Do you or have you at any time lived in an environment like my military training?

Be encouraged. You can come from there into a great place of satisfaction and encouragement. You are the maker or breaker of this part of your manhood!

When you're not encouraged it's harder to do your best. But it's not too late to turn it around.

Hope you get my point about encouragement. You won't see anyone go backwards with it!

I've never seen a bloke – or a woman – go backwards with encouragement!

A Watto Tip: Empower the woman you love.

Encourage from the heart

Encouragement from the head is good, but whatever courage it may take for you to give it out of your *heart* will result in a win! Gold!

Come on, how much does it cost to talk to someone? You can do it. Let the words flow from your heart, especially to the girl of your dreams.

Just a friendly nod, or a genuine, 'Good morning', or 'Have a great day' can lift a person's attitude. We can't get inside someone's head so we'll never know what's going on in their life. One word at the right time can really make a difference.

This is a gem from the *Work Manual*:

> And let us consider how we may spur [encourage] one another on toward love and good deeds. (Hebrews 10:24 NIV)

That is, lovingly encourage others to 'extract the digit' and make it happen.

Remember: Encourage, encourage, encourage. We can change the world for the better with this one. It beats criticism and judgement any day of the week.

Champions, this is another favourite of mine from the *Work Manual*: **'Do not hold back encouragement from those who deserve it when it is in your power to act'** (Proverbs 3:27). How good is that!

I want to repeat this one. **'Do not hold back encouragement when it's within your power to give it.'** So come on, let's do it.

Fellas, the more we learn to give and receive encouragement the more we get to experience that place of being a satisfied bloke in all areas of our life.

> I'm greatly encouraged by the fact that you've got to this point in my book!
> I know that your life is going to be more exciting, and richer with the girl you love
> – or the girl you are going to love.

> You're going to have great and encouraging conversations with all who pass your way.

Because you pursue living the right way, you're on your way to being a very satisfied bloke. Inside your heart and soul, you will be bubbling over with joy. How good!

Praise your woman and she'll fly you to the moon! Criticise her and you won't even get off the ground.

The power of encouragement

One of the most encouraging things over the last 14 years doing Shed Happens, with blokes all around our country, is to see men who have come from hard times and dirty places emerge open and free and real.

They can do this because they come to know who they are and Whose they are – they discover they belong to the Big Fella.

The proof is in the pudding for them as they get on with their lives. They help put love into the lives of others who are in similar places to where they've come from.

They become lifelines of encouragement for those who feel like they are sinking. Gold!

These champion men don't need any fanfare or pats on the back. They just get on with life. They are so grateful to know the inner joy that comes from the Big Fella. It can carry them through any battles that life may throw at them in the future.

These blokes are carriers of hope.

If you're ready to look at the spiritual part of who you are, add the Big Fella's power, strength and hope to your encouragement. It goes into hearts and souls to meet the deepest needs in others.

It's pretty faddy these days to have a special day for this or that community project or cause. I reckon every day should be an Encouragement Day. If we could encourage someone every day, we'd have a fantastic world.

Have a read of this little beauty from the *Work Manual*:

**Be strong and courageous.
Do not be afraid.
God is with you wherever you go.
(Joshua 1:9 Watto Version)**

When we **encourage** somebody we actually **empower courage** into that person to get on with something positive in their life. When they encourage us, we are empowered with courage – so let's make sure we start with the girl of our dreams.

Here's another beauty from the *Work Manual*:

Therefore encourage one another and build each other up, just as in fact you are doing.
(1 Thessalonians 5:11 NIV)

When anyone asks me, 'How are you going today?' my reply is, 'Bubbling over with joy!' If you answer in this way too, I guarantee you will get a smile and a positive response. Try it, it's a winner.

One of my mates said he'd been thinking about me for the past 2 days so he gave me a call. That's a good thing to do when God puts someone on our mind.

Give 'em a call and have a mini Shed talk. We listen, we ask, we encourage, we pray for each other for our needs, and we thank God for his provision. Boy, it's encouraging. I try to keep up the coffees, the brekkies, the footy catch-ups and whatever I need to do to encourage my buddies 'cause they encourage me.

Everyone wins with encouragement.

But, champions, for real-deal dinky-di love, the stuff that never fails, the first person on your list of people to encourage is the girl of your dreams – the others will fit in and flow. No encouragement to your girl, and the rest will show up as not the complete deal. Mate, you are the maker or breaker of this.

I've never seen anyone go backwards with encouragement.

TO REMEMBER

Encouragement comes easier to some of us than others, but it's OK, you can learn it.

Once you learn to give it, eventually it will come back to you in bucket loads.

No 'fluffy duck' patronising stuff. Start small, and keep it real.

I've never seen a bloke or a woman go backward with encouragement!

Share the joy!

Champions, I hope you've enjoyed the journey of Learning to Love – whether it's been a little bit of learning or a lot. I hope you've picked up a few gold nuggets and that you've been encouraged to take them into your heart to pass on to the girl of your dreams, or the one you are yet to meet.

I reckon every bloke who reaches a point of knowing and experiencing the Big Fella's real-deal dinky-di love also knows about the amazing feeling of inner **JOY. It's a place of peace and satisfaction amid all circumstances**, where God's love reigns over all. It's where the power of love wipes away the love of power.

To have been in love with Margaret for over 50 years has been my greatest joy, and being a father is not far behind.

How about you? What have been some of your main moments of joy so far?

Fellas, welcome to this place of JOY. IT'S MORE THAN BEING HAPPY.

Joy is not just a girl's name! Joy is about knowing the real guts of who we are. Joy is available to every one of us.

Joy replaces bad things and sad times, and the regrets and pain of deep hurts. I want to finish my book at a place of deep joy. In fact, I want you to know that joy is there for you and me no matter what battle or challenges we may be facing.

You can create moments of joy in the battle – or you may just need to become more aware of the moments of joy you are already having.

When I spend time with any of our 6 grandchildren – from the 2 year old up to the 18 year old – we can be doing quite simple things together. No matter what we're doing, the connection with them brings joy that flows into my heart and soul. How good is that?

Champions, avoid isolation. If you try to do life without people, you make it very difficult for joy to flow in. Healthy connection with others helps kick loneliness and depression. Let the joy flow in so you can let the joy flow out to all those around you.

When I was a boy, joy for me was having an ice cream, a now-and-then special treat. I had no idea that joy could be something you could have all the time!

The world needs heaps and heaps of joy. Why have we made it so rare?

Champions, all the way through my book I've passed on my favourites from the *Work Manual*. I don't just want to tell you about them, more importantly I want to **show you how to live them God's way in your day-to-day**.

This promise from the *Work Manual* is a little beauty for me:

> *'Pursue righteousness,' said Jesus, 'and be satisfied.'* **(Matthew 5:6)**

In other words, pursue His way of living and be a satisfied bloke.

Fellas, it's not about 'religion'! You don't find satisfaction deep within your heart and soul from chasing rituals, traditions, or stuff that's human-created.

It's possible to **know the words but not be able to sing the songs**. We can sit in church, go through the stuff, and not meet Jesus. Don't fall for diversion, just go straight to the top and hang out with the Creator of the universe. How good! He'll keep you in tune!

I am satisfied. I know who I am and Whose I am. My heart and soul are free and clean. I'm in a great place. Hope you are too.

I choose to do a thing we could call 'right living' to the best of my ability. That doesn't mean I'm 'always right'! It's doing life the Big Fella's way from the promises in his *Work Manual*, and seeing His Son, Jesus, as my true-to-life present-day lifestyle coach.

You will know by now that I choose to accept the spiritual part of who I am, so I have my heart and soul open to a constant flow of God's joy coming into my being. **The best way to get more joy is to keep it flowing out to others.**

Whether you accept the spiritual part of you is your call. Don't be pushed or rushed either way.

I've discovered that real-deal joy comes from going after God's goodness and ways. How's this gem from the *Work Manual*:

> **This is a sacred day before our Lord. Don't be dejected and sad, for the joy of the Lord is your strength!** (Nehemiah 8:10 NLT)

If you chase after grubby stuff for joy it will eventually come back to bite you big-time and shrivel you up inside, leaving you joyless. I want you to get all the facts so you can make a choice. It's your call!

Champions make it happen!

Fellas, I hope you've enjoyed this journey with me in my book. What I've told you isn't what **I've heard about from others, but from the hard yards I've done in all areas of love.**

I'm so glad that I came to know the spiritual part of who I am because that has enabled me to tidy up all my past stuff-ups and given me freedom in my heart to love Margaret. Looking back over the years I can see why we did things at different stages of our love and marriage which made a good and significant difference.

We were always committed to making our marriage work, so when we made mistakes, we could say sorry and make it happen again.

I reckon that learning how to love, especially our woman, is really one of the most important things we get the opportunity to do in our life. You don't have to blow it!

Love never fails.
That's the real-deal stuff made in heaven.
Remember, when the power of love
        is in absolute control of the love of power,
then it's going to go fantastic.

If you can't walk with her, you can't dance with her!

Margaret and I are the
        makers or breakers of our marriage.
It's the same for you if you want it.

Margaret and I have never been into wanting some kind of fairytale marriage. We just wanted to get on and make it real for us.

But once again, if you want a fairytale marriage, it's up to you to make it happen. **Over our journey of love Margaret has made me her hero and I have made her the most important person in my life.**

Go for Gold. Go for God. The *Work Manual* is the true heart manual with plenty of gold to help you learn to love and be loved by a woman.

It all happens in your heart.

Champions, I hope you've enjoyed our learning to love journey in my book. I hope you can take what may work for you, give it a crack, re-jig it and/or delete it, reshape it to fit for you and get on with your life.

All the best with the new, real-deal dinky-di love that's made in heaven. It's the stuff that never fails and gets better and better.

See ya in the Shed someday. Keep amazing, and have fun!

Every Bloke's a Champion... Even You!

IAN 'WATTO' WATSON

'I've never seen a bloke go backwards with encouragement.'

Finances, fatherhood, divorce, depression, anger, broken dreams. The modern male has a lot to contend with. But Watto says every bloke's a champion, even you—and he means it. His straightforward words-from-the-heart help men achieve the turbocharged life they've dreamed of but never thought they could have.

Ian has a wonderful knack for telling it how it is. Andrew Ireland, CEO Sydney Swans football club

This book is for you, champ, whoever and wherever you are.
Phil Smith, ABC Radio 'Weekends with Phil'

This book is written from real life experience in a language the average punter can understand with stories we can relate to.
Paul Morrison, Chaplain, West Coast Eagles football club

Watto will encourage your heart and put a fire in your belly.
Peter Janetzki, Talking Life, Radio 96five

The stuff Watto talks about will help set you free... it did for my husband, and in doing so, has revitalised our marriage.
Julie Oster, Farmer

Pick up Watto's book, have a read and let change begin. Timothy Nagel, Airline Pilot

'Champion, I'd love to meet you at Shed Happens!'

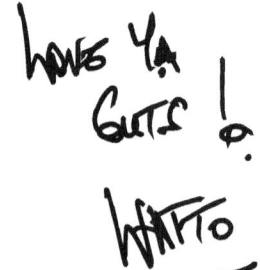

the championsguide.com

Champion Blokes 'Shed' Their Shame!

'There's no shame in shame. It has a go at every man, woman and child at some time in our lives. This book is a gutsy, hands-on way to freedom and victory.'

Watto tackles the topic that nobody wants to talk about, but everybody battles with: shame. Painful events in Watto's own childhood created a shame that hung on deep inside and held him back. It took him 50 years to recognise it, and deal with it. Now he wants to help other men kick pain, shame and sadness, and be free in a new way.

In *Champion Blokes 'Shed' Their Shame!*, Watto tells his own and other blokes' real-deal stories of escaping the prison of shame. This book will help men heal from their own mistakes and the mistakes of others, and start living the turbocharged life.

Watto ... goes for the guts of his passion – seeing men free from the rubbish and lies that have held them back from becoming the real deal blokes they were created to be. Paul 'Morro' Morrison, Chaplain, West Coast Eagles

In-your-face honesty with real-life facts and spiritual wisdom that can help you find healing in areas that you didn't even know healing could be found. Dr Fred Gollasch, Teacher, Educator, Mentor and Co-Founder of Better Blokes

shednight.com